Preserving Childhood for Children in Shelters

Preserving Childhood for Children in Shelters

Edited by
Thelma Harms,
Adele Richardson Ray,
and Pam Rolandelli

CWLA Press
Washington, DC

CWLA Press is an imprint of the Child Welfare League of America, Inc.

The Child Welfare League of America (CWLA) is a privately supported, nonprofit, membership-based organization committed to preserving, protecting, and promoting the well-being of all children and their families. Believing that children are our most valuable resource, CWLA, through its membership, advocates for high standards, sound public policies, and quality services for children in need and their families.

CHILD WELFARE LEAGUE OF AMERICA, INC.
440 First Street NW, Third Floor, Washington, DC 20001-2085
E-mail: books@cwla.org

CURRENT PRINTING (last digit)
10 9 8 7 6 5 4 3 2 1

Cover design by Sarah Knipschild
Text design by Sarah Knipschild and Steve Boehm

Printed in the United States of America
ISBN # 0–87868–612-6

Library of Congress Cataloging-in-Publication Data

Preserving childhood for children in shelters/edited by Thelma Harms, Adele Richardson Ray, and Pam Rolandelli.
        p.   cm.
    Includes bibliographical references.
    ISBN 0-87868-612-6 (ppk)
        1. Homeless children --United States.   2. Shelters for the homeless--United States.   I. Harms, Thelma.   II. Ray, Adele Richardson.   III. Rolandelli, Pam.
    HV4505.P74   1998
    362.73'2--dc21   98-18708

CONTENTS

ACKNOWLEDGMENTS

We gratefully acknowledge the Hasbro Children's Foundation, which in the early 1990s funded a project in North Carolina to provide in-service training for people serving young children in shelter settings. The project, Respite Child Care for Children in Crisis, was the first in our state to conduct a survey of shelters serving families with children, to hold a statewide conference for 100 shelter staff members on meeting the needs of children in shelters, and to provide on-site in-service training and consultation. That project, codirected by Thelma Harms and Debby Cryer of the Frank Porter Graham Child Development Center, University of North Carolina at Chapel Hill, was the genesis of this book

We particularly appreciate the inspiration and guidance given to the initial project by Rachel Fesmire, head of Family and Children's Services, Greensboro, North Carolina.

Bringing this book to a successful conclusion was not easy and took the devoted perseverance of Adele Richardson Ray and the outstanding editorial skills and personal commitment of Steve Boehm of the Child Welfare League of America to keep the book on track.

Ultimately, it was the many shelter staff members in North Carolina—who participated in the initial project, reviewed drafts of various chapters of this book, and continue to serve children—who inspired us to undertake this book.

Thelma Harms
Adele Richardson Ray
Pam Rolandelli

INTRODUCTION

Preserving Childhood for Children in Shelters

Thelma Harms

Childhood is the time of most rapid growth—physically, mentally, and emotionally. Patterns develop during childhood that influence attitudes and achievements throughout a child's life. In this volume, we discuss what shelters can do to preserve childhood for their young residents, whose development has been put at risk.

The term *shelter* has no clear definition. Generally, it means something that covers or provides protection—for our purposes, a temporary haven for people in crisis. We know that some shelters are designated for homeless people and others for victims of family violence. These two types of shelters have many similarities. Many women with children who are victims of family violence find themselves in shelters for homeless people. Shelters for victims of family violence also have to deal with the reality that their young residents have been abruptly forced to leave behind everything in their familiar surroundings. The adults often need to find new and independent ways of life.

Shelters typically house many strangers in close quarters; they are under stress, and so is the staff. Shelters often operate in make-do environments and with unstable funding. The challenges admittedly are great, but the needs of the residents and the dedication of the agency and staff are even greater. Chapter 1, "The Effects of Homelessness on Children and Families," and Chapter 2, "Children and Domestic Violence: Recognizing Effects and Building Programs," set forth the basic challenges we face as we try to serve homeless families and victims of family violence in the shelter environment.

Although serving parents in shelters is important, meeting the needs of their children is just as important. Shelters do not address children's needs directly—almost as if they operate on the premise that by meeting the needs of the parents, the parents in turn will be able to meet their children's needs. But childhood passes quickly, often too quickly for burdened parents to help their children make optimal use of their early years. The premise of this volume is that shelters serving families should consider children their clients equally with parents.

What is required to provide a good quality of life for children while they are in shelters? Protection, supportive relationships, and appropriate cognitive stimulation are the three basic components. Protection includes health, safety, and prevention of abuse or neglect. Children in shelters often lack adequate primary health care, such as protective inoculations. They are at increased risk for contracting infectious diseases because of their cramped living quarters and repeated exposure to strangers. The common environmental safety precautions required to protect young children, such as gates to prevent falls from staircases, often are absent from shelters. Moreover, the adults in their environment, including their own parents, are under tremendous stress, which may lead to neglectful or punitive behavior toward children. Chapter 6, "Health Problems of Children in Shelters," and Chapter 7, "Support and Education Programs for Parents," focus on the protection of children in shelters.

The emotional foundations laid in childhood are the basis for a healthy self-image and the ability to relate well to others. Children need accepting, secure relationships with parents and other adults in order to build emotional resilience. In the midst of the disruption that usually accompanies shelter residence, parents often find themselves without the emotional resources for parenting, which puts additional strain on caregivers. Shelters therefore must be prepared to provide support and guidance for parents and caregivers so they, in turn, can support children. Chapter 4, "Choosing and Supporting Shelter Caregivers," explores the role of the caregiver in a shelter child care facility; Chapter 7, "Support and Education Programs for Parents," discusses working with parents.

Finally, children need well-equipped supervised places to play, with safe, appropriate toys and activities. Play is a natural way for children to incorporate their experiences and develop concepts and skills. Supervised, well-appointed places for children to play indoors and outdoors typically are not available in shelters. In a 1990 survey of 118 shelters in North Carolina, 40% of the 76 shelters responding reported no outdoor play areas, and 41% reported no indoor play areas [Cryer & Harms 1990]. Parents were the most frequently reported supervisors (89%); only 11% of the shelters reported that they had paid supervision or volunteers. Only 14 of 52 shelters responding (27%) had child care facilities.

Many shelters are housing families for relatively long periods of time, even though they were designed as minimal, short-term facilities for single adults. Chapter 3, "Creating Environments for Play," explores aspects of play space; and Chapter 5, "Developing Activity Programs for Children in Shelters," discusses curriculum. In addition, Chapter 7, "Support and Education Programs for Parents," describes many attributes of a good shelter child care center.

Shelters must accomplish many crucial functions behind the scenes, such as funding and using volunteers successfully. These two functions are discussed in Chapter 8, "Volunteers in Programs for Homeless Children," and Chapter 9, "Funding." And because shelter providers are always ready for inspiration and information, Chapter 10, "Programs for Children in Shelters: An Overview," offers several short descriptions of successful programs, illustrating different approaches to offering services.

Whatever we can do to help children and parents function competently while they must reside in shelters makes a significant contribution to their well-being and can avoid problems. We add power to what we do by providing guidance to parents to help them become self-sufficient, productive adults and good parents. Shelters are a current necessity, but our goal as a society should be to make them obsolete. As long as we do need them, however, we should use shelters as an opportunity to afford children in crisis a place to be children— a protected place to play, learn, and feel secure—a place to learn that life can be better.

Reference

Harms, T., & Cryer, D. (1990). *Survey report. Services to families and children in North Carolina shelters.* Chapel Hill, NC: Frank Porter Graham Child Development Center, University of North Carolina at Chapel Hill.

The Effects of Homelessness on Children and Families

Janice Molnar

> For nine months, the infant grows and grows in the womb, in a way grows rather ironically: the quarters are limited. [A]t the end...the small but developed body [is] quite bent over on itself and cramped; yet so very much has happened—indeed, a whole new life has come into being. For some hundreds of thousands of American children that stretch of time, those months, represent the longest rest ever to be had, the longest stay in any one place [Coles 1970: 3].

The disappearance of the crisis of family homelessness from daily headlines has fostered a certain complacency among policymakers and a sense among the public that the problem is no longer with us. Contrary to what the lack of media attention may suggest, however, family homelessness is anything but over.

Homelessness is both an old and new problem. Although the vocabulary has changed, some people have always been without a permanent place to call home: vagrants, hoboes, runaways, waifs, and even witches [see Beard 1987]. It is also a new problem in terms of the composition of the homeless population and the huge numbers of families who have lost their homes. Fifteen years ago, this nation began to see the largest incidence of family homelessness since the Great Depression [McChesney 1993]. During the 1980s, the numbers skyrocketed. In New York City in 1978, about 800 families were in emergency shelters. This number had more than tripled to 2,500 by the end of 1983 and doubled again to a peak of over 5,000 in the summer of 1987 [New York City HRA 1988]. In King County, Washington, the demand for emergency shelter for families more than tripled during the 1980s [Seattle Emergency Housing Service, n.d.]. These examples were more than regional idiosyncrasies; unfortunately, they represented national trends. In a five-year period in the mid-1980s, the U.S. Department of Housing and Urban Development found that, nationwide, the number of family shelters more than doubled from 1,900 to over 5,000 [Rog et al. 1995].

Since the early 1990s, the numbers have stabilized at an unconscionably high level, although there is no agreement on a total count. Best estimates of the number of homeless people nationwide range from 250,000 to 3 million [Rossi 1990]. Estimates of the numbers of homeless families vary just as widely. Jencks [1994] estimated that in March 1990, 324,000 people were homeless in the United States, including 53,000 members of families with children. In its annual survey of member cities, the U.S. Conference of Mayors has found consistently higher numbers. According to its most recently released report, families with children accounted for 38% of the homeless population in the 29 cities surveyed [U.S. Conference of Mayors 1996]. Some observers estimate that the percentage of homeless families is even higher in rural areas than it is in cities [Vissing 1996].

What happened in the last decade to produce this juxtaposition of deep social distress against a backdrop of expanding wealth in the United States as a whole? Quite simply, growing rates of poverty during the 1980s combined with shrinking housing options and an unsympathetic federal administration to batter relentlessly our nation's families, putting them in an ever-precarious position. In that period, the policies of the Reagan Administration took root and were reinforced by the Bush Administration. The 1990 recession only made things worse, and it is more sobering still to contemplate the future effects of the recent dismantling of the nation's welfare system.

For example, consider the housing statistics.[1]

- Five million American households pay more than half of their incomes on housing.

- Between 1973 and 1987, the median price of a house rose by more than 20%, while median family income rose by less than 1% and actually fell for the poorest fifth of the population. In the same period, rental costs rose 13% faster than inflation.

- Breaking a 50-year tradition that began with the Federal Housing Act of 1937, the Reagan and Bush Administrations cut support for subsidized and public housing programs by 80%.

- In 1995, fewer than one in five families on welfare received housing assistance. In 1996, funding for the development of new public housing was completely eliminated.

---

[1] The housing and poverty statistics cited here are largely drawn from reports produced by the Children's Defense Fund [CDF 1996; Johnson et al. 1991; Mihaly 1991], the National Center for Children in Poverty [1996]; and the National Coalition for the Homeless [1996].

At the same time:

- Since 1979, the number of low-income families with children has risen precipitously—in part because of rising unemployment and underemployment, and in part because of cuts in federal entitlements. In 1994, more than 15 million children, or 21.8%, lived in families with incomes below the poverty level.[2] For children under age 6, the rate is higher still. In 1979, 3.4 million young children, or 18% of children under age 6, lived in poverty. By 1994, the numbers had swelled to 6 million children. This translates to 25%—one in four—of our nation's youngest children.

- Among 18 industrialized countries, the United States has the highest rate of child poverty.

- During the 1980s, 2 million relatively secure, well-paying jobs disappeared per year in steel, textiles, and other industries. Nearly half of all new jobs created in the same period were far less secure and paid only minimum wage.

- While the stock market has boomed and the assets and incomes of a narrow band of elite workers has grown substantially since the early 1980s, family incomes in the lower- and middle-wage brackets have stagnated. Between 1973 and 1993, workers in the highest-income families saw their annual earnings grow by almost 3%, whereas those with the lowest incomes saw theirs fall by almost 12%.

- Between 1970 and 1990, benefits provided by Aid to Families with Dependent Children (AFDC) fell by 39%, after adjusting for inflation. Currently, the combined value of AFDC and food stamps is below the poverty level in all 50 states.

- The recently signed law overhauling welfare removes the 61-year-old federal guarantee of cash assistance for low-income children and, according to analyses conducted by the Urban Institute, will send an estimated 1.1 million additional children into poverty [Zedlewski et al. 1966].[3]

---

[2]   In 1996, the federal poverty threshold was $15,141 for a family of four.

[3]   In 1996, President Clinton signed into law a sweeping reversal of six decades of federal policy. Replacing AFDC, Temporary Assistance to Needy Families removes the federal guarantee of cash assistance for poor children, requires welfare recipients to go to work after two years, creates a lifetime five-year limit on benefits, and penalizes states that fail to move 25% of their welfare caseload into jobs within a year.

Who Are Homeless Families?

Although the demographics vary from region to region, homeless families can be found throughout this country. University of Missouri sociologist Kay Young McChesney [1992] has identified four basic types of homeless families:

- **Families** in which the primary breadwinner, usually a former blue-collar worker in a declining industry, is unemployed. A significant number of these families have moved from the Rust Belt to the West, where they can be found under expressway ramps living in tents or automobiles.

- **Single mothers with children,** who have recently left relationships with men on whom they were economically dependent.

- **Long-term welfare recipients** unable to pay their rent.

- **Young mothers who have aged out of the foster care or juvenile systems**—that is, formerly homeless teenagers.

To these four categories can be added two others:

- **Young mothers who have lived with their families of origin and have never lived independently.** Frequently, the birth of a baby leads to their being turned out by their families.

- **Political and economic refugees** who lack legitimate access to public benefits.

As the demographics vary, so too do the needs and capabilities of homeless families. For some, the bottom line is that they need housing, period. Other families may need services like job training and child care along with housing so they can get jobs and maintain their housing once they get it. Still other families may need much more intensive interventions—like drug counseling, mental health services, or homemaker services—to enable them to live independently.

To a large extent, there is no single profile of a homeless family, and the designation "homeless" is artificial in its implication that homeless families are somehow different from other low-income people—or even from others who do not live in poverty. Housed families, through some crisis, become homeless; homeless families, with the right kinds of support, can become rehoused. In short, the problems of many homeless families are the same as those facing other low-income people. Homelessness is but a point along the continuum of poverty.

Nevertheless, even considering the fluidity of the population and the crossover of families from housed to homeless to housed again, the differences between the chronic unrelenting demands of poverty and the acute crisis of homelessness may be significant and enduring. What, for example, is the impact of the insult of homelessness on the family and its ability to cope? What does the physical and emotional disruption of existing social networks, family routines, and emotional grounding in one's own home do to families, and what does it take to get reorganized and restabilized? In particular, how does homelessness affect young children? Will the experience so disrupt their lives that its impact will stay with them in the long term? Unfortunately, data on the impact of homelessness on young children are sparse; but what there is, is troubling.

Impact on Health

"Gloria" and her family share a room in a former tourist motel in New York City, now operated by a voluntary, not-for-profit agency as a shelter for families. At 2 1/2, Gloria is small for her age. She does not talk a lot and still speaks in two- and three-word sentences, but she always has a smile on her face. She is active; plays well independently; and especially enjoys feeding, rocking, and dressing baby dolls. Severe diarrhea, however, keeps her from attending child care regularly. She has been hospitalized three times in the last five months—twice for dehydration from diarrhea and once for worms. Gloria has infant twin sisters; one twin has been hospitalized since birth with a birth defect. One weekend, all three children were admitted to the hospital: Gloria for dehydration, one infant awaiting surgery to correct the birth defect, and the other with double pneumonia.[4]

Although, as noted above, there is no single profile of a homeless family, many of Gloria's family's experiences are typical of other homeless families with children. The average family has two to three children, usually young.[5] Homeless children are sick at rates many times higher than average children, and their illnesses often go untreated until they become serious or even life-threatening. For example, uncontrollable diarrhea is common in young homeless children. A 1986 survey of families applying for emergency shelter in New York City, conducted by the East Harlem Interfaith Welfare Committee, showed

---

[4] This profile was developed from participant observation data collected at a family shelter in New York City [Klein 1987]. It is a profile of an actual child; only her name has been changed.

[5] In part, this is due to common shelter rules that restrict the ages of children who may stay in the shelter. Older children, especially boys over age 10, are often sent to live with relatives or are living in foster homes. The proportion of homeless families who report one or more children living elsewhere range from 25% to 50% [Cowal et al. 1996].

that out of 54 households surveyed, 30 children had been diagnosed with diarrhea as a diet-related problem [Dehavenon 1987]. Diarrheal dehydration is the leading cause of death among children worldwide, killing 3 million yearly [UNICEF 1989]. And although it is traditionally thought of as a disease endemic to underdeveloped, impoverished nations, we find it in the richest city in the richest country in the world.

Infants are at risk even before birth. In the only known study of birth outcomes of homeless pregnant women living in family shelters, the New York City Department of Health reported that in 1985 more than half had minimal or no health care—twice the statewide rate [Chavkin et al. 1987]. Consistent with the consequences of poor pre-natal care, one in six infants (16.3%) born to mothers living in wel-fare hotels from January 1982 to June 1984 were of low birthweight. This was more than double the rate of 7.4% for low-birthweight in-fants born to all other mothers in New York City during this period, excluding those living in housing projects, and 7.0% for the entire state of New York State at that time [CDF 1988].

Finally, in reviewing infant mortality rates, the same study docu-mented an alarmingly high rate of 24.9 per 1,000 among their home-less sample. This was half again as large as the rate of 16.6 in the public housing group, and more than double the rate of 12.0 for all other babies born in New York City during the study period.

Infants who do survive, and their older siblings, will be vulnerable to unsanitary and overcrowded living conditions, inadequate nutrition, and poor access to health care—all of which create ideal conditions for the quick spread of infectious diseases. According to data collected by the National Health Care for the Homeless Project in 19 major U.S. cities, compared with a national sample of the ambulatory pediatric population, homeless children from birth to age 12 are twice as likely to be treated for minor upper respiratory infections and ear infections, at least 3 times as likely to be treated for gastrointestinal problems, 4 times as likely to be treated for skin ailments, and 10 times as likely to be treated for poor dental health [Wright 1991]. The same patterns of illness have been reported in local studies conducted in Seattle and New York City [Miller & Lin 1988; Redlener 1988; Scanlan et al. 1988].

The inadequacy of preventive health care further jeopardizes children's health and increases the potential for more serious illnesses. For example, a study conducted in the Seattle area found that nearly 60% of a sample of 158 homeless children living in shelters had no regular health care provider [Miller & Lin 1988]. These figures are al-most identical to those from a study of 61 children in a San Diego shelter, in which 56.7% had no regular source of health care [Hu et al. 1989]. Moreover, the San Diego study found that increased dura-tion of homelessness was correlated with poorer reported health of the children. A New York City study of families with a pregnant mother or newborn who was eligible for food through the federally funded Special Supplemental Food Program for Women, Infants, and Children found that only 44% of 385 homeless families seeking emergency shelter were receiving benefits, compared with 60% of 83 families randomly sampled from the citywide public assistance population [Knickman & Weitzman 1989]. Numerous studies have documented serious problems of under- or nonimmunization among homeless children, ranging from 27% to 51% [Alperstein et al. 1988; Miller & Lin 1988; Redlener 1988]. In a New York City study of immunization rates, which included a comparison group in low-income housing, medical researchers found the rate of delayed or missed immunizations among the homeless children (27%) to be three times as high as among the comparison group (8%) [Alperstein et al. 1988]. The implications for children's health are grave indeed.

Impact on Developmental Status

In addition to the impact of homelessness on the physical well-being of children, constant upheaval, disorganization, crowded and chaotic living conditions, and literally no place to call home must take a heavy psychological toll. Yet, there is little systematic information on the cognitive and socioemotional impact of homelessness on children. Among the small number of studies that do exist, few examine the impact of homelessness compared with the risks associated more generally with poverty. Fewer still focus on very young children.

Probably the best-known and most comprehensive data come from the work of Harvard University psychiatrist Ellen Bassuk, who assessed a sample of 156 children living in 14 Boston shelters. Half of the school-age children showed signs of clinical depression and anxiety serious enough to require psychiatric referral and evaluation [Bassuk & Rubin 1987]. Most had entertained, at one time or another, suicidal thoughts. According to their mothers, 43% had failing or below-average grades in school, 25% were in special education, and 43% had already repeated a grade. Among the 81 preschool-age children whom Bassuk tested, 47% exhibited at least one serious impairment in either language, social skills, or motor development, as measured by the Denver Developmental Screening Test, an instrument frequently used by pediatricians to identify gross delays. Among a comparison group of 75 preschoolers from low-income families, the rate was only 16% [Bassuk & Rosenberg 1988].

Using a different battery of instruments, a Philadelphia study also documented significantly more developmental delays—especially in receptive language and visual-motor development—among 40 homeless 3- to 5-year-olds than among a comparison group of 20 children of the same ages in low-income housing [Rescorla et al. 1991]. In a New York City study, however, comparing 81 homeless and 70 3- to 5-year-olds in low-income housing, both groups were developmentally delayed [Schteingart et al. 1995]. Using the Early Screening Inventory to assess developmental status, the study found no significant differences in language, cognition, perception, or gross and fine motor between the two groups. Both groups performed poorly: Overall, each was about a year behind the level of development ordinarily expected for children their ages.

On behavioral and emotional indicators, the Philadelphia study found a higher incidence of such problems as anxiety and depression among the homeless preschoolers than among those who were housed. Based on the Child Behavior Checklist (CBCL), a parent-report behavioral checklist, 20% of the homeless preschoolers—compared with 5% of the low-income housed children—exhibited behaviors of a serious enough nature and frequency to suggest the need for mental health intervention. A somewhat different pattern of results emerged in the New York City study, as well as a Minneapolis-based study of 159 homeless 8- to 17-year-olds and a comparison group of 62 low-income housed children of the same age [Masten et al. 1993]. Both of these studies found more similarities, as measured by the CBCL, than differences between the housed and homeless groups. Even though the homeless children were reported to have more problems than the housed children, these differences were not significant. Both homeless and housed children exhibited a higher prevalence of behavioral and emotional problems than the general child population.

These studies suggest a continuum of vulnerability and cumulative risk. They raise deep concerns about the conditions to which children are exposed living in shelters. Shelters are frequently dirty, scary, overcrowded, and violent places. For children for whom homelessness is more than a temporary condition—especially for children whose families move from one shelter to another—many may be at risk of developing mental health problems that will interfere with their long-term growth and development.

The data reported by these and other studies are reinforced by observational data and by teachers' accounts of homeless preschoolers in 14 early childhood programs in New York City and a Maryland Head Start program [Molnar et al. 1988; Koblinsky 1996].[6] Especially notable are the following types of behaviors:

---

[6]   For the other studies referred to here, see reviews of the impact of homelessness on children by Molnar et al. [1990], and Rafferty and Shinn [1991].

- **Immature large or gross motor behavior.** This is especially evident in a clumsy stride and awkwardness when running.

- **Short attention span, weak impulse control.** The child is restless, has difficulty sitting still, and cannot focus on an activity without constant one-on-one attention from an adult. She seeks attention through testing or acting-out behavior.

- **Withdrawal.** The child isolates himself from the group. His emotions are flat, and he engages in thumb sucking and other self-stimulatory behavior.

- **Aggression.** The child has a low threshold for frustration. She is prone to tantrums, is quick to overreact, and is actively intrusive.

- **Regressive behavior.** This is toddler-like behavior among preschool-age children, such as thumb sucking and other oral behavior, mouthing and sucking of toys, and hoarding food and toys.

- **Sleep disturbances.** The child has difficulty getting to sleep, is restless when trying to sleep, experiences disturbed sleep, and has difficulty awakening.

- **Speech delays.** The child has little expressive language. His speech is garbled; he slurs his words and is difficult to understand.

- **Inappropriate social interaction with adults.** The child is demanding and testing, not trusting on the one hand, yet indiscriminately seeking of attention and affection on the other. She is ambivalent or avoidant toward her mother.

- **Immature peer interaction.** He is unable to share or to take the perspective of another and is easily frustrated by his peers.

- **Strong sibling relationships** (contrasting with immature peer interaction). The child displays strong bonding, empathy, and protective tendencies, and precocious, sometimes even developmentally inappropriate, caregiving behaviors in her relationships with younger siblings and parents.

This litany of negative behavior can too easily lead us to ignore the incredible resilience and positive coping strategies of children who live in truly stressful situations, and points to the necessity of interpreting behavior appropriately. The strengths and the adaptability of children's coping strategies are too often masked by behavior that is traditionally considered inappropriate. What may be judged as inappropriate behavior may be quite appropriate once the context of the behavior is better understood. For example, the physical activity and running around that is frequently characterized as hyperactive may be quite an appropriate antidote to a small, cramped, and crowded living space. Awkward gross motor movements should not be surprising among children who, as infants and toddlers, are either held or confined to strollers. A roaming toddler demands boundless energy and attention from adults. In most shelters, however, the halls are unsafe, the floor is dirty, and a small room—if one is lucky enough to have a room— cramps free movement. The safest and clearest choice for the mother, under such conditions, is to prohibit the child's movement. Unfortunately, the practical short-term solution can lead to impaired psychomotor development.

The state of the art of developmental assessment provides its own opportunities for misinterpreting children's behavior. One key issue is the extent to which traditional assessment batteries assume previous exposure to the many toys and trappings of a middle-class childhood. Only the most careful and sensitive assessments can disentangle whether observed deficits are the result of impaired cognitive functioning or, quite probably, whether they reflect the lack of relevance of certain concepts in the child's everyday world. With this population in particular, however, it is important not to project additional deficits onto a group of children already suspected of experiencing considerable developmental lags—and by doing so, to ignore potential strengths.

The Importance of Child Care for Children in Crisis

Appropriate and timely intervention with children and their families is the most effective way to support families and keep them from losing their bearings altogether. The powerful potential of high-quality early childhood programs—especially for young, at-risk children—is well documented [Bronfenbrenner 1974; Consortium for Longitudinal Studies 1983; Gomby & Larner 1995]. The New York City research cited above documented consistently higher scores on the Early Screening Inventory (ESI) for children—both housed and homeless— who had the advantage of as little as three months of exposure to early childhood education in either Head Start or publicly funded day care [Schteingart et al. 1995]. Moreover, the longer a child was enrolled in an early childhood program, the better the child's performance on the ESI. Such data show that early childhood education for impoverished young children substantially increases developmental competence, as measured by observable, age-appropriate behaviors.

Certain bottom-line practicalities also argue for early childhood programs for young children living in family shelters or transitional housing facilities. Supervised child care is essential to enable parents or caregivers to seek or meet the demands of employment, attend school or training, fulfill welfare obligations, and seek permanent housing. A 1985 survey of 154 mothers living in four New York City welfare hotels found that 90% expressed a need for child care. Their reasons for needing care included housing search (64%), public assistance appointments (63%), medical appointments (49%), job search (42%), food stamp appointments (38%), shopping (28%), and other miscellaneous reasons [Vanderbourg & Christofides 1986].

How can day care help the child? If homelessness is characterized by chaos, instability, violence, and lack of control, then a child care program, to be a suitable antidote, has to be safe, predictable, and nurturing. The antidote for a chaotic environment is an environment that is not overstimulating—one that, for toddlers and preschoolers alike, is built around a nurturing, homelike routine that incorporates sleep time, food preparation, and wholesome meals. A structured, predictable environment is essential to counteract the effects of instability. To counteract lack of control, an early childhood environment must offer choices within limits. And to counteract rootlessness, the program should help the child create a sense of belonging and personal space.[7]

Supports for Family Functioning

Children's developmental status cannot be considered separate from the available supports for the family unit as a whole. As one shelter provider in New York City has described it, the child's behavior is directly related to the parent's functioning and stability:

> After being here a while, a mother gets very angry and depressed. The child mirrors the mother's stress; the child's behavior reflects the mother. It's not clear whether the behaviors a child exhibits are related to homelessness per se, or to the mother's state.[8]

Although the average length of stay in family shelters has increased over time, most facilities are short-term in duration and thus targeted at families' immediate needs. Few have the resources to respond to the more complex and long-standing problems that families may have. Moreover, programs vary significantly in the range of services they provide. Many do not even serve the whole family. In 16 of the 29 cities

---

[7]   See Klein et al. [1993] for a practical illustration of these points.
[8]   The provider quotes in this section are taken from Molnar [1988].

surveyed in the U.S. Conference of Mayors' most recent assessment of hunger and homelessness, families may have to split up to be sheltered [U.S. Conference of Mayors 1996]. This kind of assault on the integrity of the family unit can threaten the coping abilities of the most well-functioning family; for those who are more fragile, their stability can be seriously undermined.

Even the best of family shelters may give subtle messages that can erode the regenerative capacities of homeless families. One mixed message advocates independence and self-sufficiency while encouraging dependence and control. In the words of another provider:

> We see the effect on the parents more than on the child. This environment is intrusive; it lacks privacy. The mothers are constantly monitored. They must check in and out; they must verify their baby-sitting arrangements. Caseworkers are always prying into their lives. Teachers know all about their children. There is little privacy. Men are not allowed in. We can see the mothers become depressed, withdrawn, angry.

Yet another provider echoed a similar perception:

> It's an unreal situation. No cooking facilities, no phone, no utility bills to budget for and pay, asking at the front desk for toilet paper. Particularly for those people who have never lived on their own, this experience does not teach independent living skills.

The experience of parenting in this context has been called a "double crisis" [Hausman and Hammen 1993]. Not only are families struggling with the trauma of losing their homes, they are also facing daunting impediments to effective parenting, as adults confront their limited capacities to protect and support their children in the most fundamental ways. An observational study of the relationship between mothers and their children staying in Atlanta shelters revealed what the researchers called the "unraveling" of the mother's role as a consequence of shelter living [Boxill & Beaty 1990]. Where once it was the mother's prerogative as to when and what to eat and where and how to secure food, clothing, housing, and health care, now it is everyone's business but hers. Shelter living seems to cause the unraveling of adult responsibility and the resumption of childlike behavior, as the adult role of "provider, family head, organizer, and standard setter" is taken over by others [Boxill & Beaty 1990].

The apparent relationship between this dependency-fostering behavior and parental depression has grave implications for the child. And depression among homeless parents is endemic. Research conducted in New York City indicated that 46% of a sample of 82 homeless mothers had scores on the Center for Epidemiologic Studies Depression Scale that indicated a need for further psychological assessment [Schteingart et al. 1995]. Research suggests that depression in parents may have particularly negative consequences for children, more so even than other forms of mental illness [Lyons-Ruth et al. 1984]. Young children, in particular, may be especially vulnerable because parental depression, with its attendant psychological unavailability, appears to be more disruptive at that early stage of development, when children normally use their secure relationships with their parents as a base from which to explore their environments.

By the time many homeless families request emergency shelter, they have exhausted all personal and family resources. In New York City, for example, 82% of the families who seek emergency shelter have come from doubled-up situations, many having stayed with relatives or friends after losing their housing [Knickman et al. 1989]. Research on the relationship between stress and social networks in the lives of low-income families indicates that stressed families with weak social supports present more psychological symptoms than do stressed families with strong social networks. In light of that finding, the results of clinical interviews conducted with homeless mothers in Boston shelters are sobering. When asked, "What people could you turn to in a time of stress?" 26% of the 80 mothers interviewed could name no one; 30% could name only one person; 26% mentioned a minor child [Bassuk et al. 1986]. The relationship between stress and social supports is complex, however. The relatives, friends, and neighbors of low-income families are themselves likely to be poor, stressed, and needing support. After being turned out by kith and kin, many homeless families simply have nowhere to turn.

Recommendations

Family shelters, transitional housing, supportive services—these are not the solutions to homelessness. Nonetheless, they offer critical opportunities for helping homeless families get back on their feet. What works best? Quite simply, the strategies that we know are most effective with other vulnerable families are appropriate here as well.

Create specially tailored interventions that address the multiple housing, educational employment, health, and social service needs of homeless families. Through a system of integrated case management that stresses outreach and coordination with community-based services, shelters can deliver comprehensive services to families experiencing a range of difficulties.[9]

Promote services that are empowering, not paternalistic, and that foster the integrity and stability of the family unit. Shelter

---

[9] See Weinreb and Buckner [1993] for a review of the characteristics of effective shelter programs for homeless families.

services and policies should promote family connections with marital partners and other relations. Keeping families intact and not requiring their separation is one basic approach. Enabling private moments is another. Family shelters should also support parents in their parenting roles by affirming their responsibility for nurturing, protecting, and teaching their children. A program can foster a climate of respect and tolerance for different child-rearing approaches—even while educating parents on alternative approaches. Programs can also empower parents by involving them in establishing rules and procedures for basic daily routines like meals and bedtime.[10]

Provide developmentally appropriate activities for children during their stays at family shelters. In addition to meeting children's nutritional and health care needs, family shelters should offer access— either on-site or off-site—to child care or early childhood education programs and to after-school programs for older children, staffed by teachers with special training to help them understand and cope with the developmental problems discussed in this chapter.

Establish a continuum of support services through relocation to permanent housing. Homeless families should not be forced to bounce from shelter to shelter because of limits on lengths of stay. Instead, specially shelters should be designated to accommodate families with children from the onset of homelessness until they are settled into permanent housing and functioning independently. Continuity and ongoing support are essential.

Leonard Stern, the founder of Homes for the Homeless, the nation's largest provider of transitional housing for homeless families, reminds us that "for democracy to work, the promise of equal opportunity must be tempered with built-in safeguards so that the most vulnerable members of the system are not excluded" [Nuñez 1996: xii]. The bottom line is that children and their families need permanent housing if they are to thrive—safe, decent housing in communities where high-quality supportive services are readily accessible. We must mobilize public will to demand far more than the incomplete policy response we have now. Until we deal with the problem of housing for the poor successfully, children will continue to become homeless and suffer the consequences.

References

Alperstein, G., Rappaport, C., & Flanigan, J.M. (1988). Health problems of homeless children in New York City. *American Journal of Public Health, 78,* 1232–1233.

---

[10] See Anderson and Koblinsky [1995] for a fuller discussion.

Anderson, E.A., & Koblinsky, S.A. (1995). Homeless policy: The need to speak to families. *Family Relations, 44,* 13–18.

Bassuk, E.L., & Rosenberg, L. (1988). Why does family homelessness occur? A case-control study. *American Journal of Public Health, 78,* 783–788.

Bassuk, E.L., & Rubin, L. (1987). Homeless children: A neglected population. *American Journal of Orthopsychiatry, 57,* 279–286.

Bassuk, E.L., Rubin, L., & Lauriat, A.S. (1986). Characteristics of sheltered homeless families. *American Journal of Public Health, 76,* 1097–1101.

Beard, R. (Ed.). (1987). *On being homeless: Historical perspectives.* New York: Museum of the City of New York.

Boxill, N.A., & Beaty, A.L. (1990). Mother/child interaction among homeless women and their children in a public night shelter in Atlanta, Georgia. *Child and Youth Services, 14,* 49–64.

Bronfenbrenner, U. (1974). *A report on longitudinal evaluations of early childhood programs. Vol. 2. Is early intervention effective?* (DHEW Publication No. OHD 74–24). Washington, DC: Office of Child Development, Department of Health, Education, and Welfare.

Chavkin, W., Kristal, A., Seabron, C., & Guigli, P.E. (1987). Reproductive experience of women living in hotels for the homeless in New York City. *NY State Journal of Medicine, 87,* 10–13.

Children's Defense Fund (CDF). (1988, January). United States' progress in saving infants' lives has stopped according to recent data. *CDF Reports, 9*(8), 1.

Children's Defense Fund (CDF). (1996). *The state of America's children yearbook: 1996.* Washington, DC: Author.

City of New York Human Resources Administration (HRA). (1988, January). *Five-year plan for housing and assisting homeless families.* New York: Author.

Coles, R.T. (1970). *Uprooted children: The early life of migrant farmworkers.* Pittsburgh: University of Pittsburgh Press.

Consortium for Longitudinal Studies. (1983). *As the twig is bent . . . lasting effects of preschool programs.* Hillsdale, NJ: Lawrence Erlbaum Associates.

Cowal, K., Shinn, M., & Stojanovic, D. (1996, November). *Parent-child separations among homeless and poor housed families in New York City.* Paper presented at the annual meeting of the American Public Health Association, New York.

Dehavenon, A.L. (1987). *Toward a policy for the amelioration and prevention of family homelessness and dissolution: New York City's after-hours emergency assistance units in 1986–87.* New York: The East Harlem Interfaith Welfare Committee.

Gomby, D.S., & Larner, M.B. (Eds.). (1995). Long-term outcomes of early childhood programs [Special issue]. *The Future of Children, 5*(3).

Hausman, B., & Hammen, C. (1993). Parenting in homeless families: The double crisis. *American Journal of Orthopsychiatry, 63,* 358–369.

Hu, D.J., Covell, R.M., Morgan, J., & Arcia, J. (1989). Health care needs for children of the recently homeless. *Journal of Community Health, 14*(1), 1–8.

Jencks, C. (1994). *The homeless.* Cambridge, MA: Harvard University Press.

Johnson, C.M., Miranda, L., Sherman, A., & Weill, J.D. (1991). *Child poverty in America.* Washington, DC: Children's Defense Fund.

Klein, T.P. (1987). [Effects of homelessness on children's development]. Unpublished raw data.

Klein, T.P., Bittel, C., & Molnar, J. (1993, September) No place to call home: Supporting the needs of homeless children in the early childhood classroom. *Young Children, 48*(6), 22–31.

Knickman, J.R., & Weitzman, B.C. (1989, September). *Forecasting models to target families at high risk of homelessness.* (Final Report, Vol. 3). New York: New York University Health Research Program.

Knickman, J.R., Weitzman, B.C., Shinn, M., & Marcus, E.H. (1989, September). *A study of homeless families in New York City: Characteristics and comparisons with other public assistance families.* (Final Report, Vol. 2). New York: New York University Health Research Program.

Koblinsky, S. (1996, September). Panel remarks. In J. Weinreb (Moderator), *Housing is not enough: Helping homeless families achieve self-sufficiency.* Symposium conducted by the Family Impact Seminar, Washington, D.C.

Lyons-Ruth, K., Botein, S., & Grunebaum, H.U. (1984). Reaching the hard-to-reach: Serving isolated and depressed mothers with infants in the community. In B. Colher & J. Musick (Vol. Eds.), *New directions for mental health services: Vol. 24. Interventions with psychiatrically disabled parents and their young children* (pp. 95–122). San Francisco: Jossey-Bass.

Masten, A.S., Miliotis, D., Graham-Bermann, S.A., Ramirez, M., & Neeman, J. (1993). Children in homeless families: Risks to mental health and development. *Journal of Consulting and Clinical Psychology, 61,* 335–343.

McChesney, K.Y. (1992). Homeless families: Four patterns of poverty. In M.J. Robertson & M. Greenblatt (Eds.), *Homelessness: A national perspective* (pp. 245–256). New York: Plenum.

McChesney, K.Y. (1993). Homeless families since 1980: Implications for education. *Education and Urban Society, 25,* 361–380.

Mihaly, L.K. (1991). *Homeless families: Failed policies and young victims.* Washington, DC: Children's Defense Fund.

Miller, D.S., & Lin, E.H.B. (1988). Children in sheltered homeless families: Reported health status and use of health services. *Pediatrics, 81,* 668–673.

Molnar, J., with Klein, T., Knitzer, J, & Ortiz-Torres, B. (1988). *Home is where the heart is: The crisis of homeless children and families in New York City.* New York: Bank Street College of Education.

Molnar, J., Rath, W.R., & Klein, T.P. (1990). Constantly compromised: The impact of homelessness on children. *Journal of Social Issues, 46,* 109–124.

National Center for Children in Poverty. (1996). *One in four: America's youngest poor.* New York: Columbia University School of Public Health.

National Coalition for the Homeless. (1996, December). *The choice is ours: Housing or homelessness.* Washington, DC: Author.

Nuñez, R. da C. (1996). *The new poverty: Homeless families in America.* New York: Insight Books.

Rafferty, Y., & Shinn, M. (1991). The impact of homelessness on children. *American Psychologist, 46,* 1170–1179.

Redlener, I.E., (1988). Caring for homeless children: Special challenges for the pediatrician. *Today's Child, 2*(4), 1–8.

Rescorla, L., Parker, R., & Stolley, P. (1991). Ability, achievement, and adjustment in homeless children. *American Journal of Orthopsychiatry, 61*(2), 210–220.

Rog, D.J., Holupka, C.S., & McCombs-Thornton, K.L. (1995). Implementation of the homeless families program: 1. Service models and preliminary outcomes. *American Journal of Orthopsychiatry, 65,* 502–513.

Rossi, P.H. (1990). The old homeless and the new homelessness in historical perspective. *American Psychologist, 45,* 954–959.

Scanlan, B.C., Brickner, P.W., Savarese, M., & Lee, M.A. (1988). *Clinical concerns in the health care of homeless persons.* Unpublished manuscript, St. Vincent's Hospital and Medical Center, Department of Community Medicine, New York.

Schteingart, J.S., Molnar, J., Klein, T.P., Lowe, C.B., & Hartmann, A.H. (1995). Homelessness and child functioning in the context of risk and protective factors moderating child outcomes. *Journal of Clinical Child Psychology, 24,* 320–331.

Seattle Emergency Housing Service. (n.d.). Program brochure. Seattle, WA: Author.

United Nations Children's Fund (UNICEF). (1989). *The state of the world's children: 1989.* Oxfordshire, UK: Oxford University Press.

U.S. Conference of Mayors. (1996, December). *A status report on hunger and homelessness in America's cities: 1996. A 29-city survey.* Washington, DC: Author.

Vanderbourg, K., & Christofides, A. (1986, June). *Children in need: The child care needs of homeless families living in temporary shelter in New York City.* Report prepared for (then) New York City Council Member, Ruth W. Messinger.

Vissing, Y.M. (1996). *Out of sight: Out of mind.* Lexington, KY: University Press of Kentucky.

Weinreb, L., & Buckner, J.C. (1993). Homeless families: Program responses and public policies. *American Journal of Orthopsychiatry, 63,* 400–409.

Wright, J.D. (1991). Poverty, homelessness, health, nutrition, and children. In J.H. Kryder-Coe, L.M. Salamon, & J.M. Molnar (Eds.), *Homeless children and youth: A new American dilemma* (pp. 71–103). New Brunswick, NJ: Transaction Publishers.

Zedlewski, S., Clark, S., Meier, E., & Watson, K. (1966). *Potential effects of congressional welfare reform legislation on family incomes.* Washington, DC: The Urban Institute.

Children and Domestic Violence: Recognizing Effects and Building Programs

Evelyn Williams, Marie Weil, and Robin Mauney

A local school bus stops at the street corner, and five children emerge into the midafternoon sunshine, walking toward home. Inside a nearby house, three women are busy in the kitchen preparing dinner together and discussing the day's activities. Suddenly a loud report echoes from the corner. The women freeze. The children run for the safety of the house. Their faces are terror-stricken as they pass through the front room into the kitchen. The mothers hug their children and retreat into the interior part of the house while a shelter advocate and another resident investigate the source of the sound.

This time it was only a car backfiring outside the door of a domestic violence shelter; but for many children, a loud report—a gun, or furniture being thrown—can signal the beginning of another episode of domestic violence. We witnessed this episode in a battered-women's shelter in North Carolina during the course of a statewide needs assessment of 58 domestic violence programs [Mauney et al. 1993]. The children's fear was palpable. The mothers' anguish was etched on each face. Shelter residents, staff members, and we knew that the backfire just as easily could have been gunfire—a prelude to the kidnapping of a child from the shelter, or an effort to coerce one of the women to leave the shelter by threatening her child. Even when women seek refuge from domestic violence by entering shelters, risks are still present, and women face terrible odds in trying to protect themselves and their children. Attempts to escape battering situations can be dangerous, since women often are at greatest risk when they try to leave [Browne 1987; Sonkin et al. 1985]. Separated battered women report being assaulted 14 times as often as women still living with their partners [Klaus & Rand 1992].

Shelter staff members work very hard to provide battered women the refuge necessary for healing and decision making. Even when the location of a shelter is a well-guarded secret, women and their children often fear discovery. They also feel fear about their futures and of the unknown. Domestic violence programs provide shelter and sanctuary, protection, time for reflection, and support groups and counseling to help women through their crises. Domestic violence programs also offer support, counseling, and care for children who often are fearful, withdrawn, or aggressive in reaction to the trauma they have witnessed.

Thousands of children every year witness domestic violence when their mothers are battered. Experts estimate that between two million and six million women are battered annually in this country [National Coalition Against Domestic Violence 1992]. These women may be single, married, or divorced. They are young, old, and middle-aged. They come from all racial and ethnic groups and all socioeconomic levels. More women require medical treatment for injuries resulting from domestic violence than from muggings, rape and auto accidents combined [Stark & Flitcraft 1988a].

When women are battered, their children are also affected. Carlson [1984] estimates that each year, 3.3 million children between the ages of 3 and 17 are at risk of witnessing domestic violence. Sometimes the children themselves are physically abused; more often, they are emotionally and psychologically abused—sometimes forced to watch their mothers being beaten [Dobash & Dobash 1979].

Domestic violence, or battering, is a pattern of coercive control that one person exercises over another. One form of domestic violence, physical assault, often leaves visible injuries and sometimes causes death. Less visible aspects of domestic violence include sexual violence, psychological or emotional abuse, and economic domination [Clearinghouse 1991]. We use the terms *domestic violence* and *woman battering* interchangeably in this chapter since women disproportionately are the victims of domestic violence [Dobash & Dobash 1979; Browne 1987]. Although child abuse and neglect may coexist with domestic violence in many families, our use of *domestic violence* refers specifically to the battering of women, usually by male partners.

Although any woman may be battered, findings show that physical battering often begins or escalates during pregnancy [Helton 1986] and that women with young children are more likely to seek services from shelters for battered women than are women without children [Layzer et al. 1986]. Researchers have found that wife battering, in addition to escalating during pregnancy, is likely to occur when children are quite young [Moore 1979]. The presence of infants and toddlers may be a major stress factor in already troubled relationships since the intensive care and attention that young children demand may consume time previously devoted to a partner.

Disagreements about child care and discipline are often, according to battered women, the focal points of arguments that lead to episodes of physical battering [Mauney et al. 1993]. Children overhearing these arguments may feel confused and responsible for the violence. Often, parents report—or want to believe—that their children do not know about the abuse. Forgetting the violent episodes or minimizing the severity of the violence often help battered women to cope with their situations and believe that their children are not greatly affected [Kelly 1988]. Men tend to deny the battering, offering justifications and rationalizations for their behavior. Ptacek [1988] offers examples from his interviews with men who batter. One man provided a "euphemistic redefinition" of his behavior: "I never beat my wife. I responded physically to her." Another explained his behavior this way:

> I was working, but I wasn't making any money...."The baby needs this and the baby needs that."...What do you want me to do, you know? We were at the table.... I just picked my plate up and threw it at her."

Although parents may hope that children are shielded from the battering, Jaffe and colleagues [1990], in their interviews with children, found that "almost all can describe detailed accounts of violent behavior that their mother or father never realized they had witnessed." Young children report watching assaults against their mothers through keyholes or windows when parents think the children are out of harm's way. Children tell of cowering in a corner of a room or on the stairs while their mothers are battered. Other times, they overhear the assault and, later, see the injuries inflicted on their mothers. Following assaults, children have been known to stand vigil until their parents go to sleep, making sure their mothers are safe and hoping the battering will not resume [Mauney et al. 1993; Jaffe et al. 1990].

In addition to observing the violence, children are vulnerable to injury when they try to protect their mothers or when they are caught in the cross fire. Young children may try to break up an assault or throw lamps or ashtrays to distract the batterer [Langley & Levy 1977; Pizzey 1977]. Infants and toddlers can be injured if their mothers are holding them during battering episodes. Children may also be struck by thrown furniture or accidentally injured if firearms or other weapons are used during attacks. Older children are especially at risk because they will often intervene directly during an assault. They report trying to use weapons against batterers or standing between their parents to protect their mothers [National Woman Abuse Prevention Project n.d.].

The Effects of Witnessing Domestic Violence

Children who witness domestic violence may be affected in numerous and complex ways. Overall, they have more physical, emotional, and academic problems than do children who are not exposed to domestic violence in their homes [Jaffe et al. 1990]. They may become withdrawn and suffer depression; or they may become aggressive, copying the behaviors of the batterers. Children can develop many functional coping mechanisms, but living in situations where their mothers are battered most often produces acute anxiety and hypervigilance to be ready for the next attack. In such a climate of fear, trust is difficult to establish and maintain. Just as they often believe that they are the cause of divorce, children often believe that "if they just behaved better" the violence would cease. They experience guilt, feeling responsible for the battering or responsible for protecting their mothers. Guilt and shame often accompany constant fear. Behaviorally, children may be aggressive or passive, they may be overachievers or underachievers. They may experience bedwetting, nightmares, and night terrors. They may have been awakened at night during battering episodes and either witnessed the battering or fled for safety with their mothers, and night may be an especially frightening time for them [Hughes & Barad 1982; Jaffe et al. 1990; Layzer et al. 1986; Moore et al. 1989; Roy 1988].

Children often fear that they or their mothers will be killed. When admitted to shelters, children often still feel the need to protect their mothers and may cling and refuse to separate from them. They may be wary of shelter staff members and may remain guarded, ready for fight or flight. They may interpret situations as hostile when no threat is actually present [Moore et al. 1989]. Shelter staff members often observe elaborate defenses that mothers and children have developed to maintain their safety, such as hypervigilance and private language codes that signal the need for safety. Mothers and children may also sleep in their clothes and keep their shoes nearby for speedy escapes. Mothers and children who have experienced domestic violence often constantly scan their environments for sight of threat, and they may interpret many normal interactions as aggression.

Torn between both parents, children may experience confusion and ambivalence. Like battered women themselves, children often do not want their families to dissolve—they just want the violence to end and for mommy and daddy to get along. When parents do separate, children sometimes blame their mothers and repeat verbal attacks they have heard their fathers use: "Well Mom, if you would just do the dishes (or clean the house, or have dinner ready on time), it wouldn't happen." Children in shelters may encourage their mothers to return home, believing their fathers' promises that the violence will end. Conversely, they may be angry with the batterers or with their mothers for tolerating the violence. They also may feel sadness and grief that their families may dissolve and their needs may not be met [Wayland n.d.; Christopoulos et al. 1987].

When there is violence in their homes, children's increased health problems can include nervousness; tiredness; lethargy; and frequent illnesses, such as colds and flu. In one study, half the infants entering a domestic violence shelter had health problems, including weight, eating, and sleep problems [Layzer et al. 1986]. For infants, living in the midst of domestic violence can disrupt normal patterns of development. Women who are traumatized by violence and the fear of repeated violence find it hard to meet the demands of infant care. Establishing routines for babies can be difficult when batterers exhibit jealousy and demand undivided attention. Because they are so often physically close to their mothers, infants are at heightened risk in domestic violence incidents.

Older children are more likely than younger children to have been exposed to domestic violence for longer periods of time. Consequently, they may have more adverse reactions, may be at greater risk for injury, and may also have developed more survival strategies than younger children. Sons may be more likely to externalize their reactions, exhibiting aggressive, acting-out behavior. One shelter staff veteran of 10 years reports that she can tell how violent the parents are by how violently their children behave in the shelter [V. Copeland, personal communication with Robin Mauney, April 20, 1994]. In her experience, male children often act out their arguments with others in the same ways in which they have seen their fathers deal with conflict or disagreements. Sadly, shelter personnel have reported incidents in which fathers have taught their sons how to beat their mothers—training them how to "keep her in line" or how to "take care of women" [Mauney et al. 1993; Roy 1988; Jaffe et al. 1990].

The effects on daughters, however, may be more subtle. Girls tend to internalize and become withdrawn and passive [Christopoulos et al. 1987; Jaffe et al. 1990; Roy 1988]. "Children's responses to witnessing their mother being assaulted by their father will vary according to their age, sex, stage of development, and role in the family" [Jaffee et al. 1990]. Other factors, such as frequency of moves, periods of time spent with relatives, separation of parents, economic problems, and the degree and frequency of violent episodes, will also shape children's experiences [Hilberman and Munson 1978; Rosenbaum and O'Leary 1981].

Despite these many effects, child witnesses of domestic violence show a remarkable capacity to adapt and survive [Peled 1993].

Shelter personnel must recognize and respect children's resourcefulness in developing strategies to cope with violence and should be
cautious about labeling behavior as a problem and trying to extinguish
it. Experienced shelter personnel argue strongly for the importance
of respecting children's coping strategies and defenses. Maintaining
regular sleeping times or other routines, for example, may be hard for
children if they have become accustomed to keeping watch and
being hypervigilant.

In many ways, children of domestic violence are not children in
the traditional sense. They are often old before their time, worn by
stress and fear. They have experienced things many adults never experience and cannot understand—nearly constant fear for their lives or
the necessity to intervene to save their mothers' lives. Children who
come to shelters cannot be expected to behave like other children their
own age—such expectations can cause additional stress. Shelter personnel must know how to support the authority and parenting of mothers, and they must understand and be able to handle a wide spectrum
of children's coping and stress-reaction behaviors.

For example, the shelter staff might want children to change into
night clothes to sleep. Some children, however, may be accustomed to
sleeping in their clothes so they can be ready to leave in the night if
they need to escape violence. Being "ready" may be an important part
of their sense of emotional control and may be a vitally important adaptive behavior. Their mothers may decide to return to the homes in
which they were battered, and the children will continue to depend on
their strategies for survival. Moore and his associates hypothesize that
"some familial and psychological factors may be protective in that they
reduce children's susceptibility to adjustment problems that may arise
as a consequence of domestic violence" [Moore et al. 1989]. These
factors include the child's interpretation or understanding of the violence, the child's sense of self-esteem and self-efficacy, the child's social problem-solving skills, and the mother's physical and psychological susceptibility. Shelter programs must keep these factors in focus
when developing services for children.

Domestic Violence and Child Abuse

Some children have been abused in addition to witnessing the battering of their mothers. These children are at greatest risk for developing behavioral and emotional difficulties [Hughes & Barad 1982; Jaffe
et al. 1990; Roy 1988]. Children are at greater risk of abuse or neglect when their mothers are battered. McKay cites a growing body
of literature indicating the linkage of child abuse and domestic violence "with each being a fairly strong predictor of the other." Examin-

ing the issue from the perspective of domestic violence, research estimates that 45% to 70% of women in shelters report that their children are abused or neglected [McKay 1994]. Stacy and Shupe found that "child abuse is 15 times more likely to occur in families where domestic violence is present" [Stacey & Shupe 1983]. If child abuse is the entry point, research indicates that almost two-thirds of abused children have mothers who are battered [Stark & Flitcraft 1988b]. Most frequently, the father or male is the perpetrator of the abuse [Cummings & Mooney 1988].

This link between domestic violence and child abuse presents a double bind for battered women who, as mothers, are expected by custom and statute to provide for the safety of their children. Battered women often are unable to do so and therefore are held liable by authorities for the abuse of their children. Battered women risk prosecution and loss of custody if they fail to protect their children. "The assumption here is that the women *allowed* their boyfriends or husbands to abuse or kill the children, that they had the power to prevent the crime but failed to use it" [Jones 1993]. In reality, mothers and their children are in this terrifying situation of domestic violence together.

Children of domestic violence are in many ways like children from war-torn countries or refugees seeking a new homeland. They adopt adult roles and behaviors quickly and carry roles and responsibilities that children should never have to carry. Shelter personnel must recognize children's survivor status and applaud their strength for both enduring and escaping the situation. Shelter personnel commonly feel great sadness and even anger about what these children and their mothers have experienced, but it is important to praise children for surviving. Children and their mothers need this validation. They *are* survivors. Mothers should not be blamed for domestic violence; they have done what was necessary to survive. The myth that battered women can control the violence by changing their behavior often governs the attitudes of family, friends, clergy, and law enforcement. Battered women and their children must understand that fathers are responsible for their own behavior. While supporting the premise that women are not responsible for domestic violence, shelter personnel can assist battered women and help them identify how they may be able to seek relief from the violence.

Concern for the safety of their children often is the impetus for women to seek refuge at a shelter. The shelter staff is then confronted with the dilemma of providing supportive services for battered women and their children and also meeting the legal mandate to report suspected abuse or neglect. When, as frequently happens, child protective service (CPS) agencies assume that women are responsible for or could have controlled the behavior of male partners who abused their children, a pattern of blaming the victim begins, which can result in investigations and possible court proceedings. Ironically, women sometimes will stay in battering situations because they fear losing custody of their children if the battering becomes known. When shelter personnel report suspected child abuse by fathers, the consequences often further disrupt families and revictimizes battered women. This risk presents another severe stressor for women: Mothers who seek help in a domestic violence shelter often feel like they are walking a tightrope, balancing the risks of losing their children, of further violence if they stay, and of reprisals for fleeing from the batterers if they leave.

Shelter personnel must balance their legal responsibilities to protect children by reporting abuse and neglect with their advocacy roles to empower and support battered women. Shelter personnel should establish working relationships with CPS authorities. Together, they should establish policies and procedures that protect children and do not further victimize women.

Shelters, Children, and Domestic Violence

Most domestic violence shelters provide safety and services in communal living situations. Because the locations of shelters are often confidential, battered women first may have to contact crisis lines, social service agencies, hospitals, or law enforcement agencies to find shelters or to obtain safe transportation. Women and their children may seek shelter for only one night to formulate plans, or they may stay in a shelter for several weeks or months. Because of the demand for space, however, many shelters limit stays to two or three months. Transitional housing and services are needed desperately so that women and their children can have safe housing for longer periods if necessary.

At a shelter, a mother and her children may share a bedroom and bathroom with another family. The kitchen is also shared, and women often rotate or share responsibilities for preparing meals. Although these communal responsibilities can provide structure and support for women in times of crisis, the situation also reminds them and their children that they are not at home. In common with homeless shelters, adolescents, especially sons, are often encouraged to seek housing with relatives or friends rather than enter shelters with their mothers and younger siblings. The typical age range for children in shelters is infancy to middle adolescence.

The decision to seek shelter usually occurs at a time of severe crisis in the family. The severity of a battering episode, an increased threat of violence, or a specific threat against the children often is the last straw that propels a woman to seek outside help and flee to a place, a shelter, that she probably knows little about and also fears.

For the children, departures may be orderly if their mothers are carrying out plans developed over time; or departures may be in haste if their mothers flee with only the clothes they are wearing at the time. Mothers often have little idea about what to expect when they enter domestic violence shelters. Their expectations may have come from media descriptions of large homeless shelters. They may be unprepared to live in such close quarters with other families also in crisis. They may never have experienced living with others from diverse racial and ethnic backgrounds. They may be unprepared for the disruption of their family routine and having to follow the expectations of communal living, such as sharing household chores and cooking responsibilities, reporting when one is expected to return, developing regular goal plans, and reporting progress.

Differences Between Children of Battered Women and Other Children in Shelters

In common with other children in shelters, children of battered women give up their homes when they enter shelters; but they may have additional stresses and concerns. They may have been targets of child abuse. While mothers are in crisis, their relationships with their children may change, and they may be less emotionally available to their children than usual. Mothers may also be physically injured, and this may interfere with their interactions with their children. They may be emotionally depressed and withdrawn. They may have literally depleted their financial resources and may have exhausted the emotional support of their families and friends as well. It is not uncommon for batterers to threaten extended family and friends, and women may find it necessary to distance themselves from their usual support systems to find safety. Underlying the crisis, however, is a long-term pattern of distress. One major national study reported:

> The women and children who came to the shelters left homes in which physical violence and emotional abuse were frequent and had persisted over several years. A few violent incidents were not enough to drive these mothers from their homes; close to half of them had been battered for more than five years, weekly or more frequently. For some of these women, battering was a daily occurrence [Layzer et al. 1986].

Mothers may also feel powerless within shelter settings and be perceived as such by their children. As they conform to the patterns of shelter life, they may lose their independence in making decisions about daily routines, child care, and child discipline. To children, entering shelters may signal the breakup or end of their families. This dissolution may be a crisis for them, even if they have wished for it, or children may feel guilty about experiencing relief after fleeing to a shelter. Older children, especially, may feel responsible for the family breakdown.

Other unique stressors concern safety and security. Children of battered women are worried about their own safety and that of their mothers. This fear is grounded in reality, and shelter personnel should respect it. Women are at greatest risk of permanent injury or death when they attempt to separate from batterers [Browne 1987; Sonkin et al. 1985]. Batterers often use the children to manipulate mothers into returning to abusive relationships. Manipulation can include taking the children without authorization, pursuing custody through the courts, refusing child support, bribing the children, and threatening them or their mothers. And if mothers do not have full custody, they may not allow their children to go to school, child care programs, or other activities outside the shelter because the children are vulnerable to "childnapping" at this time. In joint-custody states, both parents are presumed to have equal rights to their children until custody is determined by a court. Many battered women therefore have limited options if their children are taken by batterers before custody is determined. In addition, children may resent the unaccustomed restrictions necessary for their protection at this time.

Programming for Children in Domestic Violence Shelters

Programs for women

Domestic violence programs are designed to help women achieve safety and decide how to stabilize their lives. These programs help women assess their situations, begin physical and emotional healing, and plan their futures. Clearly, planning is much more complicated when battered women are accompanied by children. Domestic violence workers, along with the staff members of family support and family preservation programs, are committed to the philosophy of self-determination and to the belief that the most important way to help children is to help their mothers toward self-sufficiency and positive parenting.

With the maturation of the battered-women's services movement, many programs are moving beyond the crisis of domestic violence and seeking ways to help women toward empowerment and self-sufficiency [Mauney et al. 1993]. Figure 1 illustrates women's basic needs if they are to move toward self-efficacy.

When women and children enter domestic violence programs, initial interventions must deal with safety and security. Women and

Figure 1.

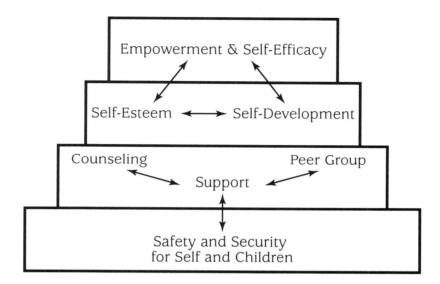

Battered Women's Needs

children need the opportunity to rest, to assess their situations, and to develop a psychological sense of safety. Once women feel that they and their children are safe, they can begin to attend to other needs, such as emotional support to overcome the psychological effects of battering. Shelter programs typically provide peer support as well as group and individual supportive counseling. The shelter experience provides space and time for women to establish peer relationships, share their experiences, learn that they are not alone, and gain support from each other as they build more positive lives. Nonjudgmental, empowerment-based counseling and support groups help women identify and explore their options. In research on domestic violence programs in North Carolina, battered women in focus groups reported that "support groups, counseling, and informal sessions with staff were the most helpful means of support. Group support from other battered and formerly battered women was described as very important in the healing process" [Mauney et al. 1993]. Supportive friendships with shelter residents, staff members, and volunteers may provide longer-term support for women as they move further in their own development. Group and individual support are also necessary for children who may not previously have had opportunities to openly acknowledge and discuss the violence in their lives.

In addition to responding to physical and emotional needs, domestic violence programs help women regain their self-esteem and begin a process of self-development. The physical and psychological assaults that women endure lead to feelings of worthlessness, systematically eroding their self-esteem. Battering is often accompanied by both public and private humiliation. Batterers often prevent women from spending time with friends and family, interfere with employment, or forbid women use of family cars. Women interviewed in our study described the shelter program as "giving them a new sense of who they were and what they could do with their lives" [Mauney et al. 1993]. With support and resources, women can regain self-esteem.

Programs typically help women to connect with educational resources, training programs, personal support groups, and counseling services. As women regain their internal resources, they are better able to resume their roles as parents. During these times of crisis, they may be most receptive to supportive interventions that can help them as they respond to their children's loss of self-esteem.

As women continue to heal, they move beyond the crisis of domestic violence and may initiate long-term plans for violence-free lives. The goal of intervention programs during these times is to help women achieve empowerment and self-efficacy.

> An exciting result that women reported from involvement in shelter programs was claiming their power as people who can make decisions, develop skills, and direct their own life choices. The ultimate goal that domestic violence programs have in providing safety and support and in building self-esteem and self-improvement is to assist women in gaining the skills and confidence to exercise their personal power so they can be effective in doing whatever they choose. This, for example, could be to pursue further education, to develop job skills, to seek employment, to relocate, and to choose friends and form relationships [Mauney et al. 1993].

Programs for children

One study indicates that 70% of women seeking shelter have their children with them, and 17% of these have three or more children [Jaffe et al. 1990]. Shelter staff members have long recognized the children's needs; but until recently, severely limited resources have constrained the capacity of shelters to respond systematically to the needs of child residents. As domestic violence programs expand beyond basic crisis and safety services, they usually begin providing children's programs as well as support groups, counseling, court advocacy, and skills training for women [Mauney et al. 1993]. Children's programs may include activities for entertainment and development, information about dealing with violence and making safety plans, developmental assessments, recreation, support groups for children, parent education, and case management.

One challenge confronting shelter personnel is the shifting membership in children's groups from day to day. Seldom will shelters have enough children of the same age for developmentally tailored experiences. A children's worker at a domestic violence shelter may have two infants, a 3-year-old, two latency-age children, and one or two adolescents one day, and a very different group the next. Not unlike the pioneer teachers in one-room school houses, children's program workers must have great flexibility and be able to develop programming that can meet multiple and diverse needs. Many of the basic principles of group work with children and early childhood education must be spliced together to create programs with the flexibility to meet the needs of very different children simultaneously. Children of all ages need opportunities to understand the nature of domestic violence; to understand that it is not their fault; to be able to talk about or play out their feelings; and to be able to express their worries, fears, and hopes.

Since lengths of stay at shelters vary, programs must be short-term oriented, and goals should be realistic for the time available. Of paramount importance is that program and staff members respect mothers' roles with their children and intervene in ways that empower them as parents. Mothers are, after all, the children's emotional anchors and primary caregivers. In many domestic violence situations, they also have been the children's lifelines. Mother-child bonds are strong. Although mothers may need help, support, and respite during these crises, staff members must acknowledge their efforts to protect their children and themselves and support their decision making. Mothers will be there for their children after their times of sanctuary in shelters are over, and their roles as caring parents must be supported and reinforced.

Longer-term support programs for children of domestic violence are needed additions to the community-based service network, but of vital importance is that all shelters develop basic programs for children for short-term crisis intervention. Appropriate objectives for children's programs in domestic violence shelters include:

- Assessing the strengths and needs of battered women and their children, and facilitating development of intervention plans, by

  Δ   providing referrals and brokering service connections as needed,

  Δ   helping mothers develop immediate plans for their safety and that of their children,

Δ   helping mothers negotiate safety plans with children's schools if necessary and strengthen their natural networks of support, and

Δ   helping mothers develop longer-term plans.

• Helping children cope with the experience of witnessing domestic violence, and beginning the process of healing by

Δ   helping them identify and label feelings,

Δ   helping them realize that they are not responsible for the violence, and

Δ   helping them develop age-appropriate and workable safety plans.

• Enhancing mothers' roles as primary caregivers of their children by

Δ   supporting their decision making;

Δ   reinforcing their roles as primary caregivers of their children;

Δ   providing parent education that encompasses basic parenting skills, helping children through the crises of domestic violence, understanding age-appropriate behavior, and using age-appropriate discipline;

Δ   modeling supportive behavior for children in crisis situations; and

Δ   providing respite services so that mothers can evaluate their families' situations, consider their options, seek the help that they need, and know that their children are safe.

To accomplish these objectives, a shelter may offer several program components or activities, including:

Crisis intervention. By the time children arrive at shelters, they may have already dealt with police in the middle of the night or waited at magistrates' offices for protective orders. Arriving at strange places and being told to settle down with strangers and adapt to new rules is confusing. Normalizing the situation as much as possible is the first task that shelter personnel face. Children must have opportunities to regain equilibrium before more structured services are offered. During initial crises, staff members provide emotional support for both mothers and children. Respite child care during this time can give battered women opportunities to gather their internal resources so they can resume their parenting roles. If resources are available, it is extremely helpful to have staff members talk with the children and comfort them while their mothers are interviewed and go through shelter intake procedures. Both the women and their children should be screened for health needs at this point.

Assessment. Within a few days, shelter personal should conduct multidimensional assessments collaboratively with mothers to determine needs and resources. Needs may include developmental assessments, health care, educational assessments, child care, social services, and mental health interventions. Shelter personnel use the assessment process as an opportunity to connect families with longer-term community resources that can be of assistance when they leave the shelter. Mothers may need assistance and support in accessing services. The assessment period can also be a time to help mothers reestablish their own support networks with such resources as family, friends, and churches. Longer-term assessment can also deal with employability, education, and skills development or training opportunities for mothers.

Emotional support. Both mothers and their children need emotional support during their time in shelters. Shelter personnel may provide children with the rare experience of receiving supportive attention to what they have endured. It may very well be the first time that children are asked to express their perspectives on what has happened to them. Staff members can use this time to help children identify trustworthy adults in their lives. If parents reunite, or if future violent episodes occur, the children will know someone to whom they can turn for help. Support may also be given in the context of children's groups, in which they are helped to identify and label feelings and deal with the fear, guilt, and confusion they may be experiencing.

Recreation. Children need safe opportunities for play. These may be provided in shelter play rooms or in well-fenced play yards at shelters, or they may be arranged in coordination with other community resources. High fences are necessary for protection and privacy. Children are vulnerable when they are away from the shelter, and efforts to ensure their safety are critical.

Modeling interactions for parents and children is an extremely important intervention. At a domestic violence program in England, one of us witnessed a young battered mother playing with her toddler in a "soft room"—furnished entirely with cushions; pillows; and safe, pliable play equipment. With encouragement from her staff worker, she began to play—swinging her baby and singing a song with her worker. After a few minutes she burst into tears and softly cried, "Why didn't anyone ever do this with me?" When families have been traumatized by domestic violence, mothers and children may not have learned how to play together. Relaxed play is a great gift that staff members can help to establish in their lives. Simple activities, like playing on outside equipment, floor games, laughing, telling stories,

and reading, are invaluable in rebuilding parent-child bonds and establishing positive reinforcing behaviors and emotions.

Staff members can also model setting limits without violence or
shouting. Women who are victims of domestic violence often have not
been good at setting limits for themselves or their children. Learning
how to respect children's needs and establish limits is an important
positive parenting skill.

Although many domestic violence shelters have very limited resources, most programs have tried hard to develop both indoor and
outdoor play areas for children. Unfortunately, the toys that shelters
receive often are old or of poor quality. Shelter staff members and volunteers should build collections of sturdy, high-quality, usable toys that
span the full age ranges of the children in their shelters.

Child care. Routine opportunities for child care services give battered women reliable times when they can attend to their own needs
and work on their plans for leaving the shelter. This regular respite
from child care responsibilities also serves as a safety valve, relieving
parental stress and enabling mothers to parent effectively. Shelters
sometimes have the resources to supply child care. If not, staff members may help mothers develop cooperative child care arrangements.
Some programs have drop-in child care centers that allow children to
stay in the facilities with day care activities for full morning programs.
When possible, centers provide these services free of charge.

In both recreation and child care programs, shelters should have
sufficient staff members and volunteers who can support developmentally appropriate activities for children of different ages and needs. This
helps children to feel security in strange settings and to begin healing.

Educational intervention. School-age children need special support at school, including arrangements for safe transportation. If children ride public school buses, shelter schedules may have to be ad-
justed so that staff members can accompany children to and from
their buses. Informing schools about specific battering situations may
be necessary so that school personnel can understand individual
children's behavior in school and provide extra support if necessary.
When sheltered children are in school, a variety of complicating cir-
cumstances may arise. Children may be forbidden to reveal the locations of their shelters, for example. Discussions with children about
this and about confidentiality for other residents is part of daily life in
shelters.

School records are public documents, and batterers can use them
to track down women and their children. When women move to other
cities, batterers often locate them through children's school records.
Schools should be made aware of safety plans; if mothers have custody orders, schools need copies so they do not release children inap-

propriately. Shelter workers often have strong relationships with local schools and day care centers and develop supportive systems to work with children from shelters.

Legal services. Children are especially at risk of being used as pawns by batterers if their mothers do not have court orders granting them custody. In many states, however, domestic violence is not considered a pertinent issue when deciding custody awards unless the children have been physically harmed or directly involved in the abuse. Judges may never hear about abuse that women have experienced when deciding who gets custody of the children. Helping mothers pursue legal options related to custody, child support, protective orders, and related matters is important in creating safe and secure environments for their children.

Parent support and education. Shelters can help mothers become better parents by offering reading materials; by providing opportunities for informal discussions with staff members, volunteers, and other parents; and through formal parent education classes. The message to battered women must consistently convey respect for their role as parents and awareness of the impact of battering on their relationships with their children. It is also important to help parents understand age-appropriate behavior for their children and how domestic violence can interfere with normal development patterns. Modeling both play with children and setting of limits can be valuable training for parents.

Principles of Services for Children in Domestic Violence Shelters

Services for children in domestic violence shelters can take many forms. Battered women and their children may also need services in shelters for homeless people. As shelters develop programs to serve children who witness domestic violence, we recommend the following principles:

- Base services on respect for the role of mothers with their children, and design them so that services strengthen, support, and enhance mothers' relationships with their children.

- During their time in shelters, children and their mothers are in crisis and are not interacting in their usual ways. Do not view their behavior through a lens of pathology. Rather, validate their strengths and resourcefulness.

- Respect, and do not try to extinguish, children's survival strategies during their shelter stays. They may need these strategies later.

- Services should be oriented for the short term, and safety should be of paramount concern. Shelter personnel should work with both mothers and children to develop safety plans to use when they leave the shelter.

- Shelter personnel should recognize the state of crisis for mothers and children and should build time into shelter schedules and daily routines for supportive recreation and relaxed parent-child interaction.

- Shelter personnel should design children's programs to support children, to allow them age-appropriate means to express their feelings about the violence in their families, to understand that there are ways other than violence to solve problems, and to support whatever strategies the children have used successfully.

- Time with staff, including just reading or talking, is valuable for many children of domestic violence. These times should be considered bona fide parts of children's programs.

- Children's program staff members must be flexible in their programming and activities for children. Because group compositions shift from day to day, activities appropriate for diverse ages are necessary.

- Many children of domestic violence will respond by becoming very withdrawn or overly aggressive. Planned activities should include efforts to draw out depressed children and calm aggressive children.

- Older children may be able to assist program staff members with activities for younger children. Staff members can model supportive behavior to help each age group. Many older children, however, have been bearing large caretaking responsibilities in their homes and may need respite from caring for younger children.

- Volunteers or shelter residents may be very helpful in supporting children's programs. Volunteers must be trained in domestic violence issues as well as child program activities. Shelter residents should work under careful supervision, with many opportunities to observe trained staff members as they work with children.

- Shelter workers should help parents connect with longer-term support programs in their communities, as well as to needed concrete services and other human services.

Figure 2.

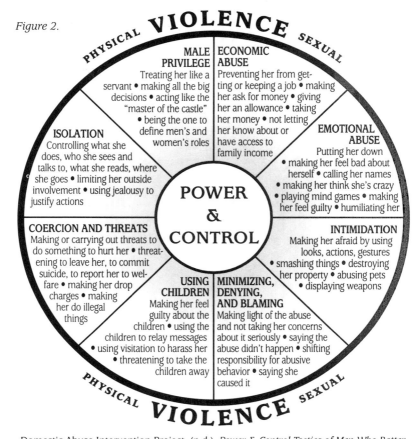

Domestic Abuse Intervention Project. (n.d.). *Power & Control Tactics of Men Who Batter* (Curriculum). Duluth, MN: Author.

- Shelter staff members should alert mothers to issues in their children's behavior that may indicate the need for longer-term support.

- Shelter staff can assist mothers in age-appropriate discipline and in understanding the impact of violence on their children's behavior.

- Shelter staff can provide both mothers and children with hope that their lives can be violence-free and that they can master nonviolent means of problem solving.

The Domestic Abuse Intervention Project in Duluth, Minnesota, a leader in the development of domestic violence programs, is also recognized as a national leader in program development for children. In its shelters, the project focuses on support, education about domestic violence, and appropriate recreation for children. Figures 2 and 3

Figure 3.

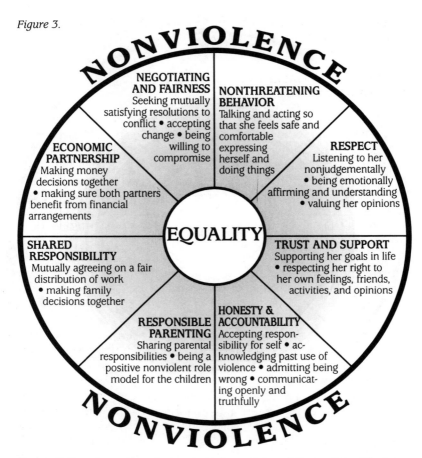

Domestic Abuse Intervention Project. (n.d.). *Power & Control Tactics of Men Who Batter* (Curriculum). Duluth, MN: Author.

illustrate the cycle of violence and abuse and the cycle of nurture. This information helps mothers understand the impact of domestic violence on children and explore children's needs for nurture and behaviors to support positive development. Aspects of this information are shared with children as appropriate.

When children leave domestic violence shelters with their mothers, they may stay with a sequence of friends, in "safe houses," in public housing, or in homeless shelters, or they may return home. Women often seek shelter three or more times before they finally leave battering relationships, and they may stay in those relationships out of fear that they cannot support their children or that their children will be taken away. Whatever the mothers' choices at particular times, children of domestic violence often could benefit from longer-term community-based support programs.

Models for Community-Based Post-Shelter Programs

As noted, children who have witnessed domestic violence often suffer emotional trauma and may exhibit a range of behaviors as a result of their experiences, from extreme shyness to a seeming ability to handle anything, from depression to aggression, from fear to bravado. All of these behaviors may be accompanied by anxiety, fear, or difficulties in trusting adults. Post-shelter group experiences with other children who have been through similar trauma can be very beneficial in helping children to heal and to practice and master more positive methods of communication, interaction, and problem solving.

In families where domestic violence is the pattern, minor disagreements or simple differences in perspectives can escalate rapidly to furniture throwing or deliberate physical injury; children often have not seen or learned respectful ways of differing and ways of listening and compromising. Communication is seriously problematic. Family members do not know how to express their needs in positive give-and-take relationships, resorting instead to communication through manipulation or threats.

To break the cycle of domestic violence and heal their wounds, children need to understand what they have experienced, and they need supportive environments in which to learn other means of communicating their needs and resolving difficulties. Social group work is one powerful intervention to break this cycle. Skill in working with children, however, is not enough to build useful post-trauma children's groups. Group leaders must understand domestic violence. They must support the rights of mothers to be their own people, respect the survival strategies that children have developed, and not "pathologize" children by focusing solely on their past traumas. Group leaders help mothers and children by using social learning processes that can heal old experiences by teaching new, positive, and supportive ways of dealing with differences.

Up to now, this need has not been recognized sufficiently. With the recent rapid growth of family resource centers and family support programs, however, it is now possible to develop nonstigmatizing programs in community settings for children of domestic violence—programs that can help build individual strengths and peer group trust. Following are descriptions of two exemplary programs that can guide other communities.

The Domestic Abuse Intervention Project of Duluth

The Domestic Abuse Intervention Project, Duluth, Minnesota, has developed an excellent manual for their post-shelter children's group program [Domestic Abuse Intervention Project n.d.] The objectives of this program include

- breaking the secret of domestic violence,
- defining violence,
- providing feeling education,
- sharing personal experiences,
- learning to protect oneself,
- having a positive experience, and
- strengthening self-esteem.

Primarily, the group program serves children ages 5–9. Children are assessed before entering, and parents participate in the assessment. Typically, a male-female team of therapists leads the group in weekly meetings over 10 weeks. Activities engage children and address aspects of their exposure to domestic violence: emphasizing that they are not responsible for the violence; helping them to express shame, isolation, and other feelings; teaching conflict resolution; and discussing issues of protection and planning. Gender roles and self-esteem are also critical components of the group's work together.

Now in operation, this model is being evaluated. Staff members are learning how to refine techniques and interventions to achieve their goals of helping children to recover from their crises and learn other means of problem solving. They believe that violence is a learned behavior that can be unlearned. The program design seeks to enable staff members to help children deal with the emotional, physical, cognitive, and behavioral effects of violence [Jaffe et al. 1990; Peled & Edelson 1992].

Parents learn about possible effects of domestic violence and are encouraged to look at how their own children have reacted to the violence in their lives. Videos, such as It's Not Always Happy at My House and The Crown Prince, often available through local domestic violence programs, can help parents understand the effects of violence on children. Support groups help children deal with longer-term emotional, cognitive, and behavioral effects of violence and to practice new behaviors. The Duluth model can be adapted easily for use in family resource centers, support programs, and schools where appropriate staff are available. Children of domestic violence can benefit greatly from nonstigmatizing ·support, education, and development activities. Domestic violence programs need to work collaboratively to plan such programs and to educate staff members in other day care, recreational, family support, and family resource programs about how to work with children of domestic violence and what special needs they are likely to have.

Group Work Program, Ontario

This program goes even further in its efforts to use well-tested social group-work theory and practice to help children who have witnessed domestic violence [Evans & Shaw 1993]. After shelter experiences, children may be referred to the Group Work Program from a variety of other programs. The Group Work Program uses prescreening and sets individual goals before placing children into the group and uses the group itself as the means of problem solving. Much attention is given to process and examining children's interaction, as well as to specific content or group tasks. The central focus is to develop children's abilities to trust the group and each other and to allow children to experience positive, supportive adults through a male-female therapist team that works well together—modeling that the children seldom, if ever, have seen.

Activities are designed so that children can learn how to communicate openly and effectively and how to understand their own and others' needs. Children have a safe place to express feelings; share their common realities; and practice new skills in communication, play, projects, and problem solving. Such longer-term, community-based efforts can help children develop more positively and give them real skills to break the cycle of abuse and violence.

The Ontario program combines models of educational groups with social learning models from social work theory. The social learning approach emphasizes more emotional involvement and can heighten learning and hasten adaptation of positive behavior [Evans & Shaw 1993]. Children of domestic violence may find it hard to become full members of a group and to get past the distrust they have learned. Activities and time to share experiences can help them overcome those obstacles. Conflict inevitably arises in all groups; in children's groups these conflicts—whether over activities, discussion topics, or general disagreements—can be used effectively to help children learn new skills and adaptive behavior for decision making and problem solving that emphasize respect for different opinions.

Evans and Shaw [1993] urge that longer-term groups for children not depend solely on educational models but rather incorporate the strengths of social group work models that focus intensively on group process, mutual aid, and social learning of more positive and adaptive behaviors. This model can be incorporated easily into programs in schools, family resource centers, and family support programs. It offers hope for learning; peer group support; and positive emotional, cognitive, and behavioral adaptations for children who have witnessed domestic violence.

The Importance of Post-Shelter Services

In an article about the Duluth Domestic Abuse Intervention Project's children's program, Grusznski and colleagues note that children often have been the forgotten victims of domestic violence [Grusznski et al. 1988]. More than 575 children have participated in the program's support and education groups for children of battered women. Evaluations have indicated promising results on several measures of success [Peled & Edelson 1992]. By the end of the program, most children can acknowledge the reality of violence in their families and understand that it is not their fault; their self-esteem has increased, they have learned new methods of self-protection, and they have increased their knowledge about formal and informal resources and supports for solving family problems.

The results of this program underscore the importance of including children's programs in all domestic violence programs, and the importance of community-based, nonstigmatizing, post-shelter services for children of domestic violence. Children should have the opportunity to recover from the crises and trauma of domestic violence. Quality programs can offer important resources toward this goal. Although many children possess great resiliency, they need emotional and educational support to cope with the traumas they have faced. Children who have witnessed domestic violence especially need nurturing and protection in a safe environment. Group programs for mothers and children can help them learn how to develop that environment. Children need adults to talk to whom they can trust. They need education and support to understand domestic violence and to learn other means of solving problems in families. Most of all, they need the opportunity to be children. Building strong children's programs in domestic violence programs, and developing strong community-based post-shelter children's groups can help meet these needs. In combination, these programs can help our society break the dangerous and destructive cycle of domestic violence.

References

Browne, A. (1987). *When battered women kill.* New York: The Free Press.

Carlson, E.B. (1984). Children's observations of interparental violence. In A.R. Roberts (Ed.), *Battered women and their families* (pp. 147–167). New York: Springer Publishing Company.

Christopoulos, C., Cohn, D.A., Shaw, D.S., Joyce, S., Sullivan-Hanson, J., Kraft, S.P., & Emery, R.E. (1987, August). Children of abused women: Adjustment at time of shelter residence. *Journal of Marriage and the Family, 49*, 611–619.

Clearinghouse on Child Abuse and Neglect and Family Violence Information (1991). *Family violence: An overview.* Washington, DC: U.S. Department of Health and Human Services.

Cummings, N., & Mooney, A. (1988). Child protective workers and battered women's advocates: A strategy for family violence intervention. *Response, 11*(2), 4–9.

Dobash, R.E., & Dobash, R. (1979). *Violence against wives.* New York: The Free Press.

Domestic Abuse Intervention Project. (n.d.). *Children's program manual.* Duluth, MN: Author.

Evans, D., & Shaw, W. (1993). A social group work model for latency-aged children from violent homes. *Social Work with Groups, 16*, 97–116.

Gruzinski, R J., Brink, J.C. & Edleson, J.L. (1988). Support and education groups for children of battered women. *Child Welfare, 67*, 431–444.

Helton, A. (1986). Battered and pregnant: A prevalence study. *American Journal of Public Health, 77*, 1337–1339.

Hilberman, E., & Munson, K. (1978). Sixty battered women. *Victimology: An International Journal, 2*(3–4), 460–471.

Hughes, H.M., & Barad, S.J. (1982). Changes in the psychological functioning of children in a battered women's shelter: A pilot study. *Victimology: An International Journal, 7*, 60–68.

Jaffe, P.G., Wolfe, D.A., & Wilson, S.K. (1990). *Children of battered women.* Newbury Park, CA: Sage Publications.

Jones, A. (1993, May). Children of a lesser mom. *Lear's, 30*–31.

Kelly, L. (1988). How women define their experiences of violence. In K. Yllo & M. Bograd (eds.), *Feminist perspectives on wife abuse.* Newbury Park, CA: Sage Publications.

Klaus, P., & Rand, M. (1992). *Special report: Family violence.* Washington, DC: Bureau of Justice.

Langley, R., & Levy, R.C. (1977). *Wife beating: The silent crisis.* New York: E.P. Dutton.

Layzer, J.I., Goodson, B.D., & deLange, C. (1986). Children in shelters. *Children Today, 15*, 6–11.

Mauney, R., Williams, E., & Weil, M. (1993). *Beyond crisis: Developing comprehensive services for battered women in North Carolina.* Winston-Salem, NC: Z. Smith Reynolds Foundation.

McKay, M.M. (1994). The link between domestic violence and child abuse: Assessment and treatment considerations. *Child Welfare, 73*, 29–93.

Moore, D.M. (1979). *Battered women.* Beverly Hills, CA: Sage Publications.

Moore, T.E., Pepler, D., Mae, R., & Kates, M. (1989). Effects of family violence on children: New directions for research and intervention. In B. Pressman, G. Cameron, and M. Rothery (Eds.), *Intervening with assaulted women: Current theory, research, and practice.* Hillsdale, NJ: Lawrence Erlbaum Publishers.

National Coalition Against Domestic Violence (1992). *A current analysis of the battered women's movement.* Washington, DC: Author.

National Women Abuse Prevention Project. (n.d.). *Fact sheet: Effects of domestic violence on children.* Washington, DC: Author.

Peled, E. (1993). Children who witness women battering: Concerns and dilemmas in the construction of a social problem. *Children and Youth Services Review, 15*(1), 43–52.

Peled, E., & Edelson, J.L. (1992). Multiple perspectives on groupwork with children of battered women. *Violence and Victims, 7,* 327–346.

Pizzey, E. (1977). *Scream quietly or the neighbors will hear.* Short Hills, NJ: Ridley Enslow.

Ptacek, J. (1988). Why do men batter their wives? In K. Yllo & M. Bograd (eds.), *Feminist perspectives on wife abuse.* Newbury Park, CA: Sage Publications.

Rosenbaum, A., & O'Leary, K.D. (1981). Children: The unintended victims of marital violence. *American Journal of Orthopsychiatry, 5,* 692–699.

Roy, M. (1988). *Children in the crossfire.* Deerfield Beach, FL: Health Communications Inc.

Sonkin, D., Martin, D., & Walker, L.E.A. (1985). *The male batterer: A treatment approach.* New York: Springer Publishing Co.

Stacey, W.A., & Shupe. A. (1983). *The family secret: Domestic violence in America.* Boston, MA: Beacon Press.

Stark, E., & Flitcraft, A. (1988a). Violence among intimates: An epidemiological review. In Haslett et al. (Eds.), *Handbook of family violence.* New York: Plenum Press.

Stark, E., & Flitcraft, A. (1988b). Women and children at risk: A feminist perspective on child abuse. *International Journal of Health Services, 18*(1), 97–118.

Wayland, K. (n.d.). *Children from violent homes.* Durham, NC: Coalition for Battered Women.

C H A P T E R

Creating Environments for Play

Thelma Harms

The environments that shelters offer children send clear messages to the families who live there about their children's worth. When shelters have good indoor and outdoor play spaces, they convey the message that they are ready for children and understand what they need. If the play spaces are supervised by trained staff members, the message is that the shelters care about children's development and are giving them the same play opportunities that other children have in preschool and child care.

When shelters that house homeless families and victims of domestic violence are prepared to treat children as primary clients along with their parents, they have an opportunity to assist parents in their child-rearing responsibilities. Supervised play areas allow shelters to use modeling as a channel for parent education.

Basically, children in shelters need both indoor and outdoor play spaces that are safe and clearly organized, that offer a variety of age-appropriate play possibilities, and that are adequately supervised. While children are in shelters, the shelters have an opportunity to give them space to play and behave like children. As they play, children can sort through distressing experiences or learn new skills, face challenges, or enjoy the comfort of repetition, depending on their needs. Play, regardless of its content, permits children to become completely absorbed in their own activities or fantasies and leave their worries behind for a time.

Playrooms

At a minimum, some clean, safe, indoor and outdoor space for play is essential for every shelter that houses children; but that goal is never easy to achieve. Creating supportive environments for play is a formidable challenge in shelters because of the pressure to use every available space for housing. Many shelters have found that playrooms located near kitchens or living rooms get lots of use because they are easy for parents to supervise while they are intermittently involved in other tasks, and they provide positive alternatives for children while parents are busy. Once a shelter takes the step and provides a play area, the obvious benefits to children and parents usually justify the use of the space. Even after the space battle is won, however, additional problems must be anticipated and solved before the play area can function well. How will the play space and equipment be kept in order and in operation? Where will the toys and equipment come from? Who will supervise the area?

Donations usually supply most of the toys and equipment needed. In fact, some shelters have so many toys donated that they cannot use them all in their playrooms and have to keep many in storage. Some of the donated toys may be unsuitable for group settings, although they were fine for individual families. For example, stuffed toys that cannot be washed are germ spreaders in group settings. If a shelter gets donations that are not suitable for the play area, or if it receives too many similar toys, they can be recycled in several constructive ways. They can be offered to shelter parents as gifts for their own children, exchanged with other shelters, or sold to buy needed equipment. One shelter, for example, sells surplus or unsuitable donated toys in a thrift shop it runs to help pay for operating expenses.

Maintaining cleanliness and order in shelter playrooms used by a number of people is always difficult. Labeling toy shelves clearly with pictures and words, and labeling boxes where different toys are kept, helps children, parents, and volunteers remember where things belong. Periodic checks by staff members or volunteers will help weed out broken toys and ensure that all the pieces are in the puzzles, that boxes still hold what the labels say, that toys are washed frequently, and that things are cleaned daily.

Who will supervise the area is another problem. In most shelters, parents must supervise their own children if they want them to use the play areas, but this approach has several drawbacks. Children cannot play when they want to but have to wait until their parents can accompany them. Parents who need respite from constantly supervising their children cannot send them out to play. Further, parents' attention is often divided between supervising their children and other activities, such as preparing meals. Employing trained people to supervise playrooms allows children to interact with adults whose main purpose is to help them gain the greatest developmental benefit from their play. If shelters cannot hire trained people, they can train volunteers to supervise playrooms on regular schedules. Parents can take turns assisting volunteers. When trained supervisors are not present, parents can, of course, supervise their own children so they can use the playroom.

Outdoor Play Spaces

Young children in shelters experience long periods of confinement indoors. They often stay in their parents' rooms in the shelters or must sit quietly with their parents while they wait in the many offices the family must visit to get help turning their lives around. Restricting young children's activity is unnatural and limiting and can lead to diminished physical coordination, lack of self-confidence, and cognitive delays. Children in shelters need safe and challenging outdoor play areas that they can use daily to counteract the confinement of living in shared, often crowded, conditions.

Good outdoor play spaces require as much planning as indoor playrooms. Play yards have to be separated from traffic and other hazards by fences. Varied ground surfaces are necessary, each suited to the play possibilities encouraged in different parts of the yard—resilient, shock-absorbent surfaces such as sand, wood chips, or rubber pads under climbing equipment; blacktop for wheel toys and ball play. Play yards should include covered areas to protect against the sun on hot days and from high winds or other inclement weather. And, of course, children benefit from having a variety of play possibilities outdoors in addition to the playground staples of climbing, ball play, wheel toys, and sandbox play. Shelters with safe, stimulating play yards should be able to answer yes to these questions:

- Are there shady places to play in hot weather?

- Are there sunny, protected places to play in cold weather?

- Is the yard surrounded with a protective barrier to protect the children?

- Are there resilient surfaces, not cement, under climbing equipment to protect children from serious injuries if they fall?

- Does the yard include play possibilities suitable for every age child, from infants through school age?

- Are there enough activities for everyone without too much waiting?

- If there are both quiet and active things to do, are these areas separated so that children in quiet play don't get run over? For example, areas for ball play should not be adjacent to sandboxes.

- Does someone check the yard daily to make sure that all toys and equipment are safe and in good repair? Are broken toys removed immediately?

- Is the yard used often for snacks or picnics, for reading stories, or for art activities and other messy play?

- Are the children watched carefully to keep them safe when they are outside? Is their play encouraged, supported, and appreciated?

Providing Child Care

Many parents in shelters need child care to free them for such responsibilities as working, attending school, looking for jobs or apartments, and obtaining medical and social services. Young children who live under the restrictions of shelter accommodations need the developmental experiences they can get from attending quality child care centers or family child care homes with ample space, toys, and trained adults as care providers. Families have to be considered individually to determine the types of programs and hours of care that best suit the needs of both parents and children.

Shelters have several options for helping parents and children who need child care. For instance, shelters may choose to help parents with transportation or other assistance so their children can continue with existing child care arrangements. Shelters may arrange with local Head Start programs, community child care centers, or several family child care homes to provide drop-in, part-day or full-time child care. Fees may be subsidized by state funds or covered by donations. Local resource and referral agencies, which have information about all licensed neighborhood facilities, are valuable resources in identifying possible care arrangements.

Some shelters offer part-time child care in their on-site playrooms for several hours each day, preferably with trained personnel heading the programs. Parents and volunteers can assist trained child care providers. The hours of care should be stated clearly, and parents should sign up their children for specified times, preferably a day in advance. The hours of service could coincide with some of the shelter programs for the parents, such as parenting classes, counseling services, or medical clinics. Some flexibility should be possible for drop-in care, but parents generally should be encouraged to plan ahead to ensure space for their children.

Shelters can provide on-site, full-time child care. Some on-site centers also care for children from other shelters in exchange for help with the operation. Taking responsibility for children in the absence of their parents takes a lot more planning and preparation than providing on-site play spaces, but the same environmental principles apply. Shelters that do provide child care must meet state licensing requirements. Most state requirements cover, at minimum, space per child, staff-child ratios, total group size, and health and safety protections. Licensing requirements for programs differ from state to state.

Licensing officials can be very helpful with funding and training resources, as well as with start-up advice.

Finally, shelters may operate off-site child care centers in cooperation with other shelters or social service agencies. Off-site centers require funding to maintain suitable licensed facilities, equipment, and staff. The Vogel Alcove in Dallas, Texas, is an example of an off-site child care center that serves children from multiple shelters. Vogel Alcove is described in detail in Chapter 10.

Guidelines for Play Environments

The following guidelines can be used for creating indoor and outdoor play areas in shelters as well as for developing child care environments both on and off the shelter site. These suggestions will help you keep the needs of the children in mind as you develop play spaces. The checklists in Appendix A can help you assess the safety of play spaces. See Chapter 6, "Health Problems of Children in Shelters," for more on ensuring children's safety.

Precautions and Supervision

Protect children with health and safety precautions and proper supervision of play.

- Make sure all toys and equipment are free of sharp edges and protruding nails and are in good repair. Better to put a toy away when it starts to break than to leave it out and risk an accident.

- Check all toys for loose pieces that could cause choking, such as eye buttons on stuffed toys, and small wheels on toy cars. Supervise carefully so that very young children do not play with toys with small pieces.

- Toys and art materials must be nontoxic, because they have a way of ending up in children's mouths.

- Wash shared toys daily with soapy water, including soft dolls and cloth animals as well as wood and plastic toys. Germs can live on toys for a long time and spread illnesses throughout the group.

- Keep indoor play spaces smoke free. No-smoking rules not only reduce the health risks of passive smoke but also prevent burns and keep cruising babies from eating cigarette butts out of ash trays.

- All surfaces under climbing equipment should be sufficiently shock absorbent, such as deep sand, thick rubber

Table 1. Recommended Optimal Staff-to-Child Ratios

Age of children	Group Size									
	6	8	10	12	14	16	18	20	22	24
Infants (birth–12 months)	1:3	1:4								
Toddlers (12–24 months)	1:3	1:4	1:5	1:4						
2-year-olds (24–36 months)		1:4	1:5	1:6						
2- and 3-year-olds			1:5	1:6	1:7					
3-year-olds					1:7	1:8	1:9	1:10		
4-year-olds					1:7	1:8	1:9	1:10		
5-year-olds					1:7	1:8	1:9	1:10		
6- to 8-year-olds								1:10	1:11	1:12

Source: National Association for the Education of Young Children. (1991). *Accreditation Criteria and Procedures of the National Academy of Early Childhood Programs* (Rev. ed.). Washington, DC: Author.

pads, or wood chips. Falls are the most common causes of play yard injuries. Children can also suffer concussions if they land too hard on their feet when jumping from heights onto hard surfaces.

- Supervise children at all times during play. Responsible adults should keep children in sight and within earshot. Safety precautions alone cannot ensure that accidents will not happen. A combination of safety precautions and careful supervision is necessary to protect children.

Ratios and Groupings

Establish adult-to-child ratios and groupings that permit individualized attention.

Children do better if they do not have to share caregiving adults with too many others, but this is especially true of children in shelters. Children who have experienced many upsetting changes, who have spent much time in confined spaces close to their mothers, and who have not had many toys to play with require more time and attention from care providers to adjust to group participation. Follow the recommendations of the National Association for the Education of Young Children (NAEYC), outlined in Table 1, for optimal staff-to-child ratios, regardless of local child care licensing regulations. NAEYC ratios most often are better than local licensing standards.

For multiage groups that include infants and toddlers, NAEYC suggests maintaining the ratios for infants and toddlers for the whole group. When infants and toddlers are not present, maintain the ratio for the majority age group. The total size for any group should be no larger than twice the staff-to-child ratio.

Decide on the best ways to group the children. If there are very few children—at most, five or six—one multiage group seems appropriate. If the group includes infants, toddlers, 2-year-olds, preschoolers, and elementary-age children, however, it may become too difficult for one person to manage alone all day, no matter how small the group. Assistants or volunteers may be necessary at certain times—as when infants are sleeping and older children need to play outside; or when all the children have to be fed, including babies who have to be held for bottle feeding. The NAEYC guidelines therefore suggest maintaining a one-to-three ratio when infants are present, or one-to-four if toddlers are present, in multiage groups. Multiage groups also require a variety of materials so that children can find age-appropriate toys. Arrange spaces to permit enough privacy and the right balance of safety and challenge for each age group.

If enrollment allows more than one group, separate the children who are still in diapers from the older children. For reasons of health, safety, and curriculum, infants, toddlers, and young 2-year-olds should be separated from other preschoolers. Age groups should have indoor and outdoor spaces suited to their own developmental levels. Separate groups for school-age children are advisable because their needs differ from those of younger children. School-age children need puzzles and games with many pieces, organized outdoor games, and places to do homework. They also need careful supervision, although the total group size can be much larger than for younger children.

Organization

Organize physical environments and materials to keep play areas running smoothly.

- Create suitable places for quiet play and noisy play, messy play and neat play, reflective play and active play. Children also need places to rest or be alone: soft areas for relaxing, protected from other children but open to adult supervision.

- Clearly separate areas where toys are used from those where toys are stored. Discourage children from playing with toys on storage shelves by suggesting that they find play spaces at tables or on rugs. Keep toys out on low, open shelves or in fairly shallow boxes so that children can reach them easily. Deep toy boxes cause children to rummage for toys and throw things out when they want things at the bottom. Toy chests with heavy lids are dangerous, as well as inconvenient for selecting toys.

- Allow children to create protected, private play spaces while they are using toys. Small rugs or mats to use as personal play areas can give them a sense of private space. Protected spaces behind low shelves and space dividers, or up in lofts, also give a sense of privacy, which is helpful for developing concentration.

- Store toys together that go together—dolls with doll carriages, crayons with paper, blocks with toy trucks or animals to use in building. The more functional the play area's organization, the more satisfying the play and the easier it is to get children and their adult supervisors to clean up after play. In larger settings, activity centers can be developed with low, open shelves to display toys, and convenient places on tables, rugs, or mats nearby for using them. Suggestions for creating activity centers come later in this chapter.

- Use picture or word labels on shelves and boxes to help children, parents, and volunteers remember where things go at cleanup time.

- Keep some safe, age-appropriate toys accessible at all times for children to select by themselves. Experiment to find out how much to have accessible. Leaving out too much leads to confusion; too little leads to lack of constructive play, lots of random running around, and conflict over toys.

- Store extra toys close at hand in activity boxes so that toys can be rotated frequently. Suggestions for activity boxes come later in this chapter.

- Have duplicate toys out so that children do not have to wait long for turns or become competitive with each other. Several small containers with crayons are better than one big box; several small boxes of Lego are better than one large set. Young children especially need duplicate toys so they can play with the same toys side by side—an age-appropriate developmental level of play for 2- and 3-year-olds.

- Create a sense of order, personal worth, and belonging by ensuring that each child has a place for keeping personal things. Large shoe boxes decorated by each child and labeled with their names, or paper or fabric tote bags made for each child by their mothers or the play supervisor, give the message that the children's things, including their creations, are important.

Rules and Routines

Establish simple rules and routines for consistency.

- Set a few simple, age-appropriate rules; state the rules in positive terms; and apply them consistently. For example: "Treat other people kindly, like friends," "Help put things back," "Respect other people's spaces and toys," or "When you are angry talk, but no hurting."

- Use waiting lists or other systems with preschoolers and older children for minimizing competition and teaching fair ways for taking turns. Make waiting lists by posting large pieces of paper low, where children can see them and put their names on the lists to save their turns. Check off names as the children finish their turns, and have them get the next child on the list.

- Make sure supervising adults know the cleanup procedures and the children's rules. Adults' responsibilities should be spelled out clearly and in positive terms. Some centers have supervising adults use guide cards that can be pinned upside down at waist height for easy reference. Volunteer or parent guide cards may include such things as

  Δ   encouragement to read to, talk to, and play with children;

  Δ   forms of discipline that are allowed and not allowed;

  Δ   where toys and games that require supervision are kept;

  Δ   suggestions on how to help children clean up; and

  Δ   requests that adults make sure things are put away properly before leaving.

- If play areas are used for child care, the routines should be fairly consistent so that children feel the support of recurring, predictable, daily structures. Meals and snacks, washing of hands, and toileting should provide pleasant and recurring events for children ages 3 to 5. Younger children should be kept on individual schedules because they are not ready for group routines. Older children may be able to handle some of the routines by themselves, once shown what is expected of them. Waiting in line during toileting and handwashing is not a good idea; have children go out for toileting one at a time. Of course, children's safety comes first—if toileting areas are not nearby, or if the children must use shared toilets and close adult supervision is necessary, group trips to the toileting area may be the only choice.

Variety
Provide a variety of materials and activities to keep children involved in constructive play.

- Include some planned activities during inside and outside play times, such as reading stories, arts and crafts, or water play with appropriate toys.

- Allow children choices among several possibilities by having more than one activity going on at all times. A variety of materials for art work, puzzles, blocks, books, carpentry, dress-up clothes, and housekeeping play should be available, although not all necessarily at the same time. Try to keep enough going on at one time to suit the group's needs, but do not let the program get overstimulating, so that children rush from one activity to the next without being able to settle down. Rotate activities and materials by using activity boxes described later in this chapter. Ideas for specific types of activities are included in Chapter 5.

- In addition to gross motor activities, make sure outdoor areas have a variety of play possibilities suitable for various ages. Activity boxes can be taken outside, with careful supervision, to allow painting, reading, or dramatic play. Ideas for outdoor fun with homemade toys come later in this chapter.

- Carefully match the size of equipment to children's ages and sizes. Infants and toddlers need very small tables, very low climbing equipment, and safe floor areas; 2-year-olds and older preschoolers also need furnishings and equipment that are the right sizes for them. The right size equipment helps children feel competent and increases independence and safety both indoors and out.

Warm Environments

Create warm, welcoming environments that make it easy for children and parents to feel ownership and involvement.

- Provide space near the children's area for parents to meet informally and socialize, with comfortable, adult-sized furniture, and coffee or soft drinks. Clothing or toy exchanges, daily newspapers, and popular magazines can be available in the parents' area. Access to sewing machines or other helpful equipment also makes parents feel supported.

- Light, cheerful colors and well-kept surfaces give a sense of cleanliness and order in both the children's and parents' areas. Have parents help, if possible, in the upkeep of the areas by painting, making slip covers, and keeping the places clean and organized.

- In large settings, managing arrivals and departures should be assigned to one of the supervising adults every day, so they are handled consistently. Extend cheerful, warm welcomes to children and parents upon arrival, and see

that children's possessions and creations are kept together for organized departures.

- Invite parents and siblings to try activities so they do not
  feel left out.

- Take pictures of children and parents to hang on bulletin
  boards and to give to them. Disposable cameras are great
  items to have, and manufacturers sometimes will donate
  them to shelters if asked.

Environments for play that make good use of space, that are safe,
that provide enough structure through predictable routines, and that
offer a variety of activities do not happen by chance. They take lots of
work and experimentation to get just the right proportions. The following suggestions on organizing activity centers, on ideas for activity
boxes, and on outdoor fun with homemade toys make for rich, stimulating environments in shelter play areas and child care programs.

Organizing Activity Centers

Activity centers are play areas that are set up with specific materials,
convenient spaces to use the materials, and clear organization so children can work as independently as possible. A carpenter's workshop
is a good guide to setting up activity centers: Tools and materials are
arranged in organized, accessible ways; work spaces are suited to the
carpenter's tasks, and cleanup tools are within easy reach.

Planning for Centers

When organizing playrooms, look first at the physical features that
cannot be changed. Note the locations of sinks and doorways, where
light shines in from windows, which areas of the room are quieter and
more secluded, and so on. Use these physical features sensibly. Try to
anticipate the flow of traffic through the room so that activity centers
will not be interrupted as children move from one area to another.
Place compatible activity centers side by side; separate centers that
are potentially disturbing to one another. Book corners are quiet areas and therefore should not go next to block or music areas. Blocks
might go well, though, near housekeeping, if teachers want dramatic
play possibilities to span both areas. Art activities go well near sources
of water for cleanup, as do cooking and science activities.

Floor surfaces should also be considered when planning activity
centers so that messy activities are in areas with floors that are easily
washable. Easily washable floor coverings are also necessary on top
of wall-to-wall carpeting wherever children will be eating or doing art
work. If possible, select floor coverings for the entire play area that

are easy to wash; for softness, provide rugs that can be picked up and washed frequently. Be sure to tape down rugs that are on slippery surfaces. Wall-to-wall carpeting, even the indoor-outdoor variety, is hard to clean thoroughly.

Selecting Activity Centers

The number of activity centers in a room depends on the size of the room and the age, experience, and ability of the children. As children progress in their abilities to select, use, and reshelve materials, their environments can offer wider selections of activity centers.

From infancy, children need safe toys and materials accessible to them on open shelves at all times for them to feel mastery over their environments and to develop independence. The correct amount of materials on open shelves differs with the age of children and their abilities to use materials independently. Infants and toddlers become overexcited when too many toys are out on open shelves. For these very young children, make duplicates of the same toys accessible, and rotate different toys frequently. By the time children are 3 years old, most can manage environments with a variety of activities arranged in activity centers that are set up clearly and functionally.

There is no list of activity centers that must be included in every early childhood environment. Supervising adults should think instead in terms of the different types of developmentally advantageous activities that should be available to children and organize these activities within the allotted space—both indoors and out. Children need books, puzzles, and other language and thinking games; blocks and building materials; creative art and music opportunities; pretend play; and active physical play.

When organizing play areas, consider the daily experiences that should go on indoors. Also think of what can go on regularly outdoors. At a minimum, arrange permanent activity centers for quiet play, active play, messy play, and noisy play. Materials and activities provided on a rotating basis in each of the four activity areas can be stored in labeled activity boxes and brought out at particular times in the appropriate areas.

Good programs will provide a number of different activities to rotate through these basic activity centers. Quiet areas should be used for books, puppets, flannel-board stories and various manipulative toys, table games, and nature exhibits; noisy areas for music, blocks, or housekeeping and dramatic play; messy areas for art, science, cooking, and sand and water play; and active areas for climbing, ball play, or dancing. Rotating different activities through these permanent activity centers during the day offers children a variety of materials, even in small settings. After a particular activity is over, materials can be put away out of sight in an activity box, and the space used for the next activity. To have several play possibilities taking place at the same time, at least one or more activities should be available simultaneously in each of the activity centers.

Visual Cues and Labeling to Promote Independence

Many play settings operate in multipurpose facilities where materials must be packed and stored. Shelves on wheels that can be rolled away with the materials stored on them are a great help in such situations. If shelves are not available to store materials, use clearly differentiated tables and boxes. Whatever the arrangement, children need to understand the system for selecting toys and replacing them. Visual cues, such as covering storage tables with red plastic, and play tables with white plastic, or putting pictures of the materials on the boxes where they are stored, helps children remember the system.

Children rely on predictable, organized environments where materials can be found repeatedly in the same places. Having boxes they decorated themselves helps children remember where their personal belongings are kept. Open storage shelves, clearly labeled with pictures and words, allow children to easily find the materials they want to play with. When shelves are clearly labeled and only a few objects are put on them at one time, putting things back in place becomes an easy task.

Adults can label block areas, for example, by cutting out the shapes of the blocks in colored contact paper and pasting them on the backs and shelves of cupboards. The backs of cabinets are ideal storage places for hanging play equipment, such as kitchen utensils for housekeeping areas, or carpentry tools, each identified by a clear outline of the object. Use pictures of games and toys to label the containers in which the toys are kept, as well as the shelves on which the containers are stored. If it is not possible to have pictures of the toys, use simple shapes such as blue circles or a red squares on both the containers and the shelves to remind children where the toys are to be returned. Clearly labeling shelves helps even very young children to become more independent in using and maintaining their environments.

Ideas for Activity Boxes

Children need so many different things to play with that keeping the things that go together in the same place can be a problem. Creating activity boxes, each filled with a different play material, is a space- and timesaving idea for organizing children's playthings.

To make activity boxes, put everything that is needed for an activity into one box. Add pictures, storybooks, and records or tapes about the activities to help the children get more play ideas. Store these boxes in closets or sheds, and bring them out when you want to use them. When the children are finished playing, they can put things back in the right boxes for next time. Label boxes clearly with large letters and pictures of the things inside.

Rotate the boxes you bring out, and each activity will seem new again and again. Here are some ideas for activity boxes you can make. Be sure all the things you put in activity boxes are safe for the children who will play with them. Before storing the activity boxes, make sure all washable toys are washed, especially those used by infants and toddlers. This cuts down on the spread of illnesses.

Infants and Toddlers

Rattles. Put rattles of different sizes, shapes, and colors into a sturdy box. Add rattles that make many kinds of sounds. Try ones that click, jingle, ring, or even have moving parts to watch. Be sure all rattles are safe and lightweight so babies can play with them on their own. Rattles should be washed with soapy water and air dried, or washed in a dishwasher, before being returned to the activity box.

Balls. Make boxes for lightweight balls of different sizes and colors. Add fuzzy tennis balls, colored shiny balls, whiffle balls, or even a few colorful beach balls.

Dump and fill. Put a few plastic bowls or plastic jars with lids in these boxes. For toddlers, add handfuls of teddy bear counters, poker chips, inch cubes, or other small safe toys to each bowl. For infants, use two-inch cubes, safe rubber squeeze toys, or tennis balls. Give each child a bowl of toys to dump and fill in his or her own special way. To prevent choking, supervise carefully so children do not put objects into their mouths.

Preschoolers and School-Age Children

Firefighting. Use old garden hoses cut into pieces, about one-and-a-half yards long, plastic firefighter hats, and a bell. Add books about firefighters, so you can read to the children to give them new play ideas.

Camping. Find canteens, knapsacks, and small lanterns in surplus stores. Put them in boxes with old binoculars and small tents made from sheets. Children will enjoy their camping play even more if you show them books about camping or tell stories about sleeping in tents on camping trips.

Store. Use clean cans (check for sharp edges), boxes, and packages from familiar items with their labels still on. Make or buy play money. Set up stores where children can "buy and sell." Let them take their things "home" to their playhouse kitchens.

Hospital. Put a few nurses' caps, stethoscopes, tongue depressors, and adhesive bandage strips into boxes so the children can play doctor and nurse. Add some books about hospitals and visiting the doctor and dentist. Use this time to talk about never taking medicines alone or playing in medicine cabinets. Do not include make-believe candy pills in hospital boxes because it gives the wrong message.

Hats. Gather several lightweight plastic and other washable hats. Make sure the hats are safe for children's play, without loose pieces that children could choke on. Choose big floppy hats, little baseball caps, hard plastic workman hats, or even cooks' hat. Try setting these activity boxes near unbreakable mirrors so children can look at themselves in the different hats. Wash the hats frequently so they will not transmit infections or head lice.

Purses, totes, and pocketbooks. Collect a few pocketbooks and tote bags of different sizes, shapes, and colors that can be easily carried around. Add a few scarves, blocks, or safe toys for young ones to put into their pocketbooks. Let them enjoy filling their bags with these special treasures or just have fun carrying them around.

Stacking. Gather things that will stack safely. Include wooden unit blocks, colorful sponge blocks, clean empty food boxes covered with contact paper, nesting blocks, or any other set of safe stackable toys. Make sure children have flat spaces large enough to build and stack, where their buildings will be safe from the active play of others.

Painters. Use white painter's caps, some large clean cans or small pails, and a few paint brushes with two-to-three inch wide bristles. The children can paint with water on the outside of the house or on the outdoor play equipment.

Travel. These boxes hold everything children need to play bus, train, boat, or plane. Put in washable uniform caps like those worn by pilots, train engineers, or bus drivers. Add tickets, paper punches, and maps. Children enjoy making trains or buses with steering wheels and boxes or chairs. They can sell tickets and pretend to take trips. Reading storybooks about travel or taking the children on real bus trips helps the play along.

Little world. Put into boxes collections of tiny cars, trucks, and little plastic people and animals. You can buy inexpensive bags of plastic cowboys and farm and zoo animals. Add small blocks for the children to build a little people world. Children can use the little world things also in three-inch deep boxes or pans lined with an inch of cornmeal or dry coffee grounds in the bottom. Terry towels placed under the pans help catch any material that may be spilled. Little-world play calms children down and is a good rainy day game.

Picture stories. These boxes hold watercolor markers, crayons, and paper. Fold the paper back about one-third from the bottom. Have the children draw pictures on the larger part of the paper, then unfold the bottom and tell you stories that go with the pictures. Print what they tell you and then read the stories back to them. Single pages can be stapled together to make books. This activity is especially good for 3- to 5-year-olds because it helps their language development and gets them ready for learning to read. Older children enjoy writing their own stories.

Gluing. Collect things of different shapes, colors, textures, and sizes that can be glued onto paper. Sort them into half-gallon milk cartons, with the tops cut off, to hold soft things, hard things, red things, blue things, shiny things, smooth things, rough things, and so on. Make up your own way of sorting. Put the filled cartons, paste or glue, and paper into activity boxes. When children work at this activity, be sure they look at and touch things in each carton. Ask them what kind of things are in each carton and help them decide how the things are alike. "In here are round things" or "This one has all the blue things."

Sorting. Fit four or five small containers, such as cottage cheese cartons or margarine tubs, into boxes so that children can sort small things. Add various collections—soft small things, buttons of all colors and shapes, tiny charms, or pebbles. Help children sort by colors and shapes, by materials the things are made of, or what items are used together. Ask them how the things they put into the same containers are the same. Be sure to keep these little things away from very young children who may put them in their mouths.

Salt-flour art dough. Make up different colors of art dough by mixing two cups of flour, one cup of salt, and one-half cup of water for each batch, and adding one teaspoon of powdered paint to the dry ingredients, or a few drops of food color to the water, as you mix each batch. Store different colors of art dough in separate covered coffee cans to keep them moist. Do not use plastic bags, because they make the art dough sticky. Children can play with the art dough, using their hands to mold and shape it. Tell the children you want to see what they can make with their hands. If you bake the shapes in a slow oven, about 250°, the dough will turn hard, and the things that children create can last a long time. The shapes make good Christmas tree ornaments or gifts.

Stringing. Put into these boxes things that children can string—old beads, sequins, soft shells with holes punched through, short pieces of plastic drinking straws, or anything else that has a hole in it and will not break. Keep the beads away from children who are too young and may choke on such small objects. Do not use macaroni or other food for stringing. To string necklaces, use coated wire from telephone cables, shoe laces, yarn, or thick string with one end wrapped in tape for ease in stringing.

Outdoor Fun with Homemade Toys

Carpentry. Use old sturdy wooden boxes, logs, or benches as woodworking tables. Provide lots of soft scrap wood, lightweight hammers, some nails, things like bottle caps to use as wheels, and small hand saws; use C-clamps to secure wood when sawing. Show children how to use these materials safely. Watch children closely when they work with carpentry tools. With close supervision, carpentry is a safe activity for children 4 years and older.

Low basketball hoops. Attach basketball hoops or old laundry baskets without the bottoms to outside walls or fences. Provide basketballs or lightweight rubber balls. Children love to "shoot baskets" if the hoops are just high enough.

Tossing targets. Cut three or four holes of different sizes in large cardboard cartons. Children can toss bean bags or small balls into the holes. Mark the ground where they should stand to toss at the targets.

Sandboxes. Lay tires flat on the ground, with plastic sheeting under them, and pour sand into the center. Several small sandboxes are sometimes better than one large one. For larger sandboxes, use truck or tractor tires. Cover sandboxes at night to keep out animals. Give children old kitchen utensils, plastic bowls, sieves, measuring cups, pitchers, or pots and pans for sand play.

Water play. Washtubs on sturdy wooden boxes make good water play tables. Give children plastic containers of many kinds to use with water—cups, sieves, and plastic bottles. Be sure to change the water each day to keep it clean. Children should wash their hands thoroughly with soap before playing in water tables to cut down on germs. Always watch children carefully around water. On hot days, let children play in sprinklers rather than wading pools, which are hard to disinfect and can spread gastrointestinal illnesses and skin infections.

Tents. Use clotheslines and old sheets or blankets to make tents between trees.

Boats. Use discarded rowboats or large cardboard boxes, or make boat outlines with logs.

Sinks and stoves. Cut holes the size of dishpans in crates; set dishpans in them as sinks. Hammer some old metal gas-stove burners onto crates, or draw burners with permanent ink markers for play stoves. Collect old pots, pans, spoons, plastic dishes, and cups to cook with outside. Keep everything close to sandboxes and water so the children can "cook." Try using smooth, short, tree stumps, large flat rocks, or smaller boxes for other pretend playhouse furniture.

Wooden boxes. Collect or build sturdy boxes the children can move around. Let them build whatever they want as long as it is safe. If the boxes stay outside, be sure to check them frequently for insects, loose boards, or nails.

Cable spools. Place small cable spools in the play yard for outdoor tables. Large spools with planks and ladders nailed to them can be used for climbing. Make sure anything used for climbing is safe and sturdy.

Knotted ropes and tire swings. Hang strong climbing ropes from sturdy tree limbs, with knots tied in the ropes at 12-inch intervals. Older children like to learn to climb ropes using the knots for foot and hand holds. Tire swings can be hung from sturdy tree limbs also. Drill holes in the bottoms of the tires for drainage.

Obstacle courses. Lay tires down, touching or with space between. Children can move along the obstacle courses, crawling or jumping from tire to tire.

Plank walks. Stretch planks between low, thick pieces of wood or low sawhorses. Tie down the ends of the planks for safety, if necessary. Children can walk across to develop balance. Offer a hand to help steady children who need it.

Good environments can only set the stage for wholesome play and constructive interaction. The following chapters deal with ways of using environments to children's best advantage by introducing teachers' roles and the curriculum for learning.

Further Reading

Cryer, D., Harms, T., & Bourland, B. (1987). *Active learning for infants.* Menlo Park, CA: Addison-Wesley Publishing.

Cryer, D., Harms, T., & Bourland, B. (1987). *Active learning for ones.* Menlo Park, CA: Addison-Wesley Publishing.

Cryer, D., Harms, T., & Bourland, B. (1988). *Active learning for twos.* Menlo Park, CA: Addison-Wesley Publishing.

Cryer, D., Harms, T., & Bourland, B. (1988). *Active learning for threes.* Menlo Park, CA: Addison-Wesley Publishing.

Cryer, D., Harms, T., & Ray, A. (1996). *Active learning for fours.* Menlo Park, CA: Addison-Wesley Publishing.

Cryer, D., Harms, T., & Ray, A. (1996). *Active learning for fives.* Menlo Park, CA: Addison-Wesley Publishing.

Frost, J.L., & Henninger, M. (1979). Making playgrounds safe for children and children safe for playgrounds. *Young Children, 35*(5), 23–30.

Frost, J.L., & Klein, B.L. (1984). *Children's play and playgrounds.* Austin, TX: Playgrounds International.

Greenman, J. (1988). *Caring spaces, learning places: Children's environments that work.* Redmond, WA: Exchange Press, Inc.

Harms, T. (1992). Designing settings to support high-quality care. In Spodek, B., & Saracho, O. (Eds.), *Yearbook in early childhood education: Vol. 3. Issues in child care.* New York: Teachers College Press.

Harms, T. (1994). Humanizing infant environments for group care. *Children's Environments, 11,* 155–167.

Harms, T., & Cryer, D. (1985). Space to play and learn. *Family day care education series.* Chapel Hill, NC: Frank Porter Graham Child Development Center, University of North Carolina at Chapel Hill.

Lovell, R., & Harms, T. (1985). How can playgrounds be improved? A rating scale. *Young Children, 40*(3), 3–8.

Choosing and Supporting Shelter Caregivers

Pam Rolandelli

At the heart of any good program for children are knowledgeable, responsive caregivers. Janice Molnar and colleagues [1988] found that participation in quality child care programs for as little as three months can begin to reverse the delays in development found in many children in shelters. Well-trained caregivers play pivotal roles in children's healthy growth and development. Choosing and supporting caregivers is critical, therefore, to successful shelter child care programs.

Hiring Caregivers

Staff composition varies according to program sizes, needs, and resources. When hiring caregiving staff members, interviewers should consider the knowledge, skills, and personal characteristics necessary to work in shelter environments.

Knowledge

- Caregivers must have working knowledge of child development and effective methods of positive discipline and classroom management.
- Caregivers should be familiar with the special needs of children in shelters and be knowledgeable about how domestic violence, child abuse and neglect, and homelessness can affect children.
- Caregivers should be familiar with current health and safety standards to help prevent injuries to children and the spread of infectious diseases.

Skills

- Caregivers must be able to plan and implement developmentally appropriate curricula, observe children's behavior, and adjust curricula or environments as necessary.
- Caregivers must be flexible and adaptable, able to change their classroom schedules at any time.
- Caregivers must possess good communication skills with both children and adults.
- Caregivers should be nonjudgmental and sensitive to the different cultures of the families in shelters. The ability to communicate with families in their spoken languages is also desirable.
- Caregivers should be able to work as team members with shelter staff members and outside agencies.

Personal Characteristics

- Caregivers should be patient.
- Caregivers should be positive and enthusiastic.
- Caregivers should take care of themselves, both physically and emotionally.
- Caregivers should be able to think and act independently.
- Caregivers should be realists, able to work with people in the real world. They should be able to accept failures and successes with equilibrium.
- Caregivers must be reliable.

This list is not inclusive, but it can help interviewers to focus on the requisite characteristics and qualifications before hiring caregivers for children in shelters.

Supporting Caregivers

The demands of working with shelter children are great and can easily lead to burnout. The book *Avoiding Burnout* lists three essential needs of caregivers that must be addressed if child care providers are to be productive and satisfied with their jobs [Jorde-Bloom 1982].

The Need for Affiliation

Child care providers need to be with colleagues who understand the day-to-day stresses they face. Creating support networks and developing community contacts will help prevent burnout and provide staff members with rich resources for new ideas.

How shelters can support caregivers:

- Develop team spirit among shelter staff by talking about shared goals, holding regular staff meetings, and maintaining open channels of communication.
- Encourage staff members to network with other caregivers serving similar populations, including other programs in the community, such as Head Start.
- Give caregivers opportunities to visit similar programs.

The Need for Achievement

Caregivers need to feel that what they are doing is worthwhile and that they are recognized for their efforts.

How shelters can support caregivers:

- Review caregivers' performance regularly and give positive feedback as often as possible.
- Provide opportunities for continuing education and training.

The Need for Involvement

Caregivers feel respected and competent when they are able to make decisions about matters that affect them directly.

How shelters can support caregivers:

- Consider delegating responsibilities to caregivers, making sure in advance this is something they want.
- Establish methods for caregivers' input into major decisions affecting them.

Minimizing Staff Turnover

Staff turnover affects program quality. To maintain quality programs, consider providing adequate pay; offering flexible scheduling; giving caregivers reasonable amounts of vacation time; providing "mental health days," allowing them respites from the pressures of caring for children; providing lounges or designated areas where staff members can relax; and training competent substitute caregivers.

The Role of Training

The National Day Care Study [Ruopp et al. 1979] and the National Child Care Staffing Study [Whitebrook et al. 1989] found that specialized training in child development and early childhood education was an indicator of staff competence and was strongly linked to the quality of programs.

There are many sources for training in early childhood education, from local workshops to graduate degrees in child development, family development, home economics, social work, or allied fields. If caregivers already have some experience and training in early childhood education when they are hired and are committed to further growth and development, reviewing current strengths and weaknesses can help determine the need for further, more specialized, individualized training.

For people who are currently employed and have little training in child care, the Child Development Associate (CDA) credential is an entry-level competency-based recognition. The program is sponsored by the Council for Early Childhood Professional Recognition and takes approximately one year to complete. For additional information about the CDA, call the Council for Early Childhood Professional Recognition at 800/424-4310.

Regardless of previous training or experience, new staff members should always receive orientations to shelter programs. An excellent resource for training staff members to work with children in shelters is *Connecting,* a curriculum developed expressly for this purpose [Ennes 1994]. Topics covered in this curriculum include

- the reality and perceptions of homelessness,
- the possible effects of homelessness on children's development,
- early childhood education applications for formerly homeless children,
- appropriate activities and materials,
- classroom management,
- serving children with special needs,
- creating multicultural environments,
- working with parents, and
- developing social service resources.

References

Ennes, J.B. (1994). *Connecting: Meeting the needs of formerly homeless preschool children.* New York: Child Care, Inc.

Jorde-Bloom, P. (1982). *Avoiding burnout: Strategies for managing time, space, and people in early childhood education.* Lake Forest, IL: New Horizons.

Molnar, J., with Klein, T., Knitzer, J., & Ortiz-Torres, B. (1988). *Home is where the heart is: The crisis of homeless children and families in New York City.* New York: Bank Street College of Education.

Ruopp, R., Travers, J., Glantz, F., & Coelen, C. (1979). *Children at the center: Final report of the national day care study.* Cambridge, MA: Abt Associates.

Whitebrook, M., Howes, C., & Phillips, C. (1989). *Who cares? Child care teachers and the quality of care in America. Final report. National child care staffing study.* Oakland, CA: Child Care Employee Project.

CHAPTER 5

Developing Activity Programs for Children in Shelters

Adele Richardson Ray

Most shelter environments are not suitable for child day care. If possible, shelters should use existing programs in the community by purchasing fixed numbers of slots or by using more suitable facilities that are not in use during the week, such as church Sunday school rooms. When child care is provided within shelters themselves, the optimal arrangements for preschool-age children are separate rooms or sections in the shelters, modified to meet the needs of preschool children and their families. (See Chapter 3, "Creating Environments for Play.")

I use the term *activity program* instead of *curriculum* because children are often in shelters for unpredictable periods of time, from several days to as long as a year. Early childhood programs for children in shelters must be prepared to meet the needs of children with a range of ages, abilities, interests, and temperaments in atmospheres of frequent stress and constant turnover.

Curriculum implies a more formal, integrated set of activities, often developed around topics or themes, and directed toward children of particular age ranges. *Activity program* is a looser term, more suited to the flexibility and adaptability of programs needed in shelters. It is unlikely that any one curriculum, even one designed for children living in shelters, could be used without some adaptation in all shelter programs. The experienced teacher should examine a variety of more general sources—such as those included in the annotated bibliography at the end of this book—to find appropriate activities, as well as curricula developed expressly for homeless children and families, Head Start migrant children, and other transient populations.

Common Needs

Regardless of age, children in shelters have common needs that planners must consider when developing activity programs.

Safety and Security

Children need to feel safe and secure. All children must be protected from adults in shelters who abuse alcohol or drugs or are aggressive toward others. Very young children, especially infants and toddlers, must be protected from older, more active or aggressive children. Safety is especially important where space is either shared or limited. Experts emphasize protecting children from the dangers of shelter environments [Gewirtzman & Fodor 1987; Molnar et al. 1988].

Implications for program planning. When selecting activities, look for books and materials that do not frighten children. Include materials that deal sensitively with children's fears and worries. Moving, fear of the dark, fear of strangers, fear of being left alone, and fear of doctors are common. Safety and security encompass how to use community helpers such as police, how to say no when necessary, and how to avoid dangerous situations. Children may have to learn how to use shared bathrooms safely, how to ask responsible adults to go with them, or how to negotiate the areas between shelters and playgrounds safely.

Privacy

Children need privacy. When children live in shelters, hotels, or transitional housing, they often have little privacy. They may share beds with other children or adults. They usually eat at tables with other families. They may not be able to find places to get away from other family members or other shelter residents. Creating even small separate places for children can give them feelings of privacy and ownership.

Implications for program planning. Whenever possible, shelter programs can give children space and materials of their own. Staff members can provide cubbies or boxes to hold children's coats or favorite toys, envelopes to store favorite pictures or stories, places to hang pictures the children have created, or desks in quiet corners. For older children, privacy may mean quiet spaces to complete homework, listen to music, or make telephone calls. Activity programs can include ideas about dressing in private or finding times and places for being alone and safe. When scheduling, include play-alone activities and activities for two or three children at a time. When necessary, plan some time during the day for brothers and sisters to play together or for families to spend private time together.

Acceptance and Respect

Children need to feel accepted and respected. Homeless children are often objects of rejection, ridicule, disgust, or pity. If they go to child care programs or attend public school with children who live in houses, they may be singled out because they are different. Because they often have little chance for outdoor exercise, they may be small for their age and awkward [Molnar et al. 1988].

Implications for program planning. Using children's names, complimenting them, listening to them, and understanding their needs show children that the adults in the shelter accept them as they are. By setting aside quiet times for conversation, programs can show children that they matter. If there are spaces for grooming, taking the time during the day for children to wash their faces and hands or to replait braids gives staff members opportunities to help children look better. In addition, program staff members can build children's self-esteem and teach them how to handle ridicule or rejection and how to stand up for themselves using words instead of force.

Success

Children need to experience success. Along with acceptance, children in shelters need to be successful. Teachers or support staff members who work with children at risk too often focus on deficits. Helping children catch up with their peers is important, but so too is finding existing strengths and building on them. Careful observation of each child's ability, temperament, attention span, and interests helps staff members choose those activities most likely to be successful for individual children.

Implications for program planning. Using open-ended materials—such as paper and pencils or crayons, Colorforms, clay, paint, stacking blocks, sand, or water—helps children experience success. If you use activities with only one right answer—such as inset or jigsaw puzzles, crossword puzzles, riddles, or dot-to-dot pictures—be certain that children can handle them successfully.

Warmth

Children need to be treated warmly, even when they themselves are withdrawn or hostile. Many children respond to the stress in their lives by withdrawing from others. They may cling to their parents, usually their mothers, and be reluctant to join other children in play. They may fear that the adults in their lives will leave them. Other children may become aggressive or hostile to create buffers between themselves and those around them.

Implications for program planning. Skilled, caring adults include these children in activities, perhaps first as observers, then as participants paired with other more active children, or in group activities such as cooking. Careful selection of books, puppets, and dramatic play activities can help children to role-play how to separate from parents and how to join groups. Puppets and dramatic play can give children props to hide behind as well as words to use in everyday situations.

Also important is planning for children who do not want to join group activities. Many children learn from watching, even when they are not directly involved. For example, children can sing songs or perform finger plays even though they watch from the sidelines and do not actually participate in the activities.

Scheduling

Scheduling activity programs in shelters requires flexibility and considering a number of issues.

Shared Space

Most shelters do not set aside spaces for children's programs. Programs for adults usually take priority, and children's programs must adapt. Staff members planning activity programs for children must therefore adjust schedules, sometimes at a moment's notice, in response to the scheduling needs of adult activities.

Since it is important for healthy child development to have predictable routines, planning with the people who will be sharing the available space is essential. It is particularly important to plan routines, especially those involving eating and sleeping, and to keep the sequence of routines intact. If children in shelters learn they will get their meals and rest periods at regular times throughout the day, they will feel that they can predict at least some part of their daily lives.

Scheduling time for use of space for exercise both indoors and outdoors is also important. If suitable space is not available inside or out, it may be necessary to use public playgrounds or gyms. This takes advance planning and may require extra help to get children there and supervise them while they are playing. In addition, this may require that some staff members remain in the center, since illness may keep some children from participating.

Hours of Operation

Unlike many programs serving children in day care settings, shelter programs may have to start later in the day and continue into the early evening. Children in shelters often sleep in the mornings because the nights are noisy and crowded, and the high incidence of chronic illnesses may cause children to need more sleep during the day. Intermittent attendance is also common because children must often accompany their parents in searching for work or obtaining social services. Children and adults should be greeted warmly whenever they arrive and return.

Using Picture Schedules

Schedules that show the main events of the day can help children feel more secure. Staff members can refer to the schedules throughout the day, both to remind children what will happen and to review what happened earlier. Large picture schedules, centrally located, make it easy for children to refer to schedules at any time.

Balancing Small Group and Individual Activities

When developing activity programs, plan both group and individual activities. For infants and toddlers, make sure each child is held and nurtured daily. Use routines like feeding and diapering to carry on conversations. Try to read to preschool children individually, as well as in small groups. Older children may want individual time to do homework or to deal with private problems, such as fears about the future or their increased family responsibilities. Try to find quiet spaces for all individual activities.

Small group activities can include cooking, art projects, listening to stories, or group discussions. Large group activities can be scheduled throughout the day for short periods of time to introduce schedules or review various events of the day. Large group activities are not appropriate for infants and toddlers. Older children should not be compelled to come to large group activities; acceptable alternatives should be available.

For those shelter programs fortunate enough to have experienced volunteers, children can receive individual attention throughout the day. If possible, try to use the same volunteers repeatedly with individual children. When volunteers are scarce, older peers or siblings can help. Setting aside times and places for older children to play with or read to younger brothers or sisters can maintain family bonds and develop individual responsibilities. Remember, however, that many homeless children act regularly as caregivers for their younger siblings and need time for their own activities.

Rest Time

A study of children sheltered at the Hotel Martinique in New York City found nap time to be especially difficult for many children [Grant 1991]. Initially, children resisted napping, often becoming disruptive. Even children who were accustomed to the hotel needed individual attention during nap time to settle down and keep from wandering. The children who had been in four or more shelters were especially vulnerable at nap time.

Shelter staff members can ease the transition for children by giving them their own blankets and sheets and letting them sleep with favorite toys or stuffed animals. Older children may want to bring books or toys with them as well. Soft music sometimes helps to set restful moods. Quiet activities should be provided for non-nappers and early risers.

Separation

Fear of separation from parents is a natural stage of child development. Separation may be particularly difficult for many children in shelters, especially for very young children or children who are frequently on the move. Many older children in shelters regress to earlier stages of development because they are under stress and fear abandonment.

Staff members must plan for separation, whether children leave shelters for other day care programs in the community or join shelters' on-site children's program while parents participate in other shelter activities. Children who attend off-site day care programs usually leave their shelters and return at predictable times. Some children who attend on-site shelter programs for children may not have predictable schedules. Their needs for day care may vary depending on their parents' schedules. Other shelters may provide regular half- or full-day child care. In any case, staff members need to be available each time children separate from their parents.

Life in shelters robs many parents of their sense of control in parenting, since they no longer do the shopping, cook the meals, or set bed times. Parents may find it difficult, therefore, to leave their children with substitute caregivers, especially if they begin to view caregivers as rivals for their children's affections.

If possible, assign individual staff members to particular children and families so that they can greet them warmly when they arrive and get the children ready to leave each day. This helps to develop relationships that, in turn, can help children prepare to leave their parents each day. One expert suggests a useful technique with infants and toddlers: Caregivers should use greeting times to learn about how the children slept and ate, how they are feeling physically, and what moods they are in [Gonzalez-Mena 1990]. Caregivers should include both parents and children in these conversations whenever possible.

Move slowly to help ease separation. Caregivers can take infants from parents after they have said good-bye. For older infants and toddlers who have trouble leaving their parents, Gonzalez-Mena suggests that caregivers try to interest the children in toys or activities in the play area. Place toys away from caregivers but near the children. If the children are especially fearful, avoid direct eye contact or physical contact until the children themselves make the first moves.

Departures may also be difficult. Some children may be absorbed in activities and may ignore parents' arrivals. Reassure parents that this is normal behavior. The last children to be picked up may become anxious and feel deserted. Try to give these children special attention, or ask older children to help organize their own belongings for easy departures.

Saying Good-Bye

Leaving is part of being homeless. In many states, children and families live in shelters for specified amounts of time and then are eligible for transitional housing. Other children have to go from shelter to shelter in the same city. Each change adds stress to the lives of children and families. Programs working with children in shelters have begun to tackle the problems of transition in various ways. The North Shore Community Action Program Head Start in Beverly, Massachusetts, has incorporated a good-bye routine that includes a story, song, and classroom discussion [Koblinsky & Anderson 1993]. Staff members display pictures of children who currently and formerly attended the shelter program: Seeing the pictures of children and families who have left the shelter program reassures children that they will not be forgotten and that there is hope for future housing.

Scrapbooks or bulletin boards with pictures of families who are leaving during the coming week help children and staff members alike anticipate transitions. Formal good-bye pictures of the whole group of children at the shelter give the families something to remember when they leave. Be sure to include favorite adults in the pictures too, such as teachers, volunteers, or other shelter staff members.

Choosing Materials

Because children in shelters vary in ages, abilities, and interests, it is important to choose materials that can be adapted to individual needs. Due to limited space in shelter programs, it may not be possible to include all the materials listed here. Make selections based on the age ranges of the children served, their cultural backgrounds, and the flexibility of use of the materials themselves. Materials that can be used with different ages of children, such as art materials, musical instruments, and balls, are especially useful additions to programs. See Chapter 3, "Creating Environments for Play," for ideas about storing materials that are not in constant use.

Many materials used in shelters are donated. Keep lists of materials you are looking for so that people who want to donate can match their donations to your needs. You may also find that local businesses can donate materials, such as paper, old envelopes, or art materials.

Whenever possible try not to use torn or dirty books or dolls, nubs of crayons, and so on, even if they are donated. Homeless children will especially appreciate having materials in good condition. As you accumulate materials, you may want to rotate them. Clear, stackable storage containers are easy for storing and identifying for future use.

Here are some examples of materials that adapt easily for use at many skill levels:

Art Materials

- Clay, Play-Doh, salt-flour art dough.
- Finger paints.
- Materials for sculptures: wood scraps, cardboard, boxes, Styrofoam, and toothpicks for construction.
- Materials for stringing: beads, bottle caps, buttons, shells—anything with a hole in it.
- Lots of paper of different sizes and colors—especially white
- Crayons; washable, nontoxic felt pens; and paints. Younger children need wider crayons; school-aged children can use the traditional narrower crayons. "Skin-tone" crayons and paints should be culturally appropriate, not just of one color.
- Chalk, chalkboards, and erasers.
- Children's right- and left-handed scissors.
- Paste, glue, and rubber cement.
- Pencils, including primary pencils for younger children.
- Magazines and catalogs to cut up for collages.

Blocks, Figures, and Vehicles

- Large assortments of wooden blocks in a variety of shapes and sizes.
- Small figures. Include multicultural figures, enough people for larger families, and older figures for intergenerational families.
- Figures depicting people with special needs, such as people in wheelchairs or with hearing aids.
- Cars, trucks, vans, boats, planes, and other vehicles. Where possible, choose vehicles with which children are familiar.
- Animals, including domestic animals familiar to the children.
- Smaller blocks such as Lego or Duplo.

Pretend Play

- Multicultural, multiracial, multigenerational dolls. Include enough dolls to make large families, and dolls representing grandparents or other older family members.
- Dolls depicting people with special needs.
- Doll beds and blankets.
- Empty food containers of healthy foods that children are familiar with and like to eat.
- A variety of pots and pans. In addition to utensils found in most American kitchens, include multicultural cooking utensils, such as woks, tortilla presses, and steamers. Base selections on the cultures of the children in the shelter.
- A variety of dress-up clothes, including ethnic clothes. Dress-up clothes should be washed weekly and should not be used when there are communicable diseases, such as ringworm or lice, which can be spread in clothing. Hats, when used, should be restricted to those that can be washed and disinfected.

Literacy Materials

- A variety of books of interest to the children, suitable for various ages.
- Hard-paged books for infants, with photographs or simple pictures.
- Flannel boards with pictures illustrating favorite stories.
- Books that deal with worries the children may have—for example, books on moving, going to school, making friends, handling emotions, facing death, dealing with divorce, or being different.
- Newspapers and magazines for adults (such as *Life, Newsweek, People, Sports Illustrated,* or *Time*); children (including *American Girl, Boy's Life, Cricket, Highlights for Children, Ladybug and Spider, Ranger Rick,* and *Sesame Street*); and adolescents (such as *Ebony, Glamour, Sassy,* or *Seventeen*).

Puzzles and Games

- Picture lotto and other matching games.
- Puzzles of varying levels of difficulty, including complicated

puzzles for older children, depending on interests and abilities.

Small-Muscle or Fine-Motor Toys

- Busy boxes for very young children.
- Pegboards, beads for stringing (large for children under age 3, to prevent choking).
- Nesting dolls.
- Coins, nuts, seeds, and buttons for sorting, with tongs to pick things up.
- Play-Doh, clay, and rolling pins.

Large-Muscle or Gross-Motor Toys

- Climbers and slides.
- Swings.
- Mats for tumbling.
- No-pedal riding toys for infants and toddlers, and safe tricycles for preschoolers; helmets for safety when needed.
- Balls in a variety of sizes.
- Hula-Hoops.
- Covered sandboxes and sand toys.
- Basketballs and goals.
- Shaded areas for hot, sunny weather—especially for infants.

Music and Videos

- Musical toys for infants: music boxes, roly-poly dolls with bells inside.
- A variety of instruments, such as bells, cymbals, and rhythm sticks. Try to include multicultural instruments, such as drums, rattles, rain sticks, cymbals, kalimbas, and gourds.
- Cassettes of music, including Ella Jenkins, Hap Palmer, Raffi, and music from many cultures.
- Cassettes of children's favorite songs, including some recorded at the shelter, based on suggestions from parents and children.
- VCRs with nonviolent story tapes.

Choosing Activities

Because children in shelters are often in multiage groups, staff members planning activity programs should be familiar with appropriate curricula for infants, toddlers, and older children. Activities should be selected based on developmental ages, relevance to the interests of children in the program, ease of setup, and availability of materials.

Nearly half of the 156 preschool children in a study of Boston shelters had serious impairments in language, social skills, or motor development [Bassuk & Rubin 1987]. Activities that combine these skills are especially appropriate in shelters. For example, rather than simply choosing to bounce balls—a motor activity—caregivers could choose activities that combine movement and music, such as bouncing balls to different rhythms; movement and language, such as bouncing *to* the chair, *across* the room, or *under* the flag; or bouncing and social skills, such as bouncing the ball to a friend. Table activities such as bingo combine listening (language skills), number recognition (cognitive skills), and learning to play with others and take turns (social skills).

Because many children in shelters have short attention spans, activities should match the attention spans of children in the program [Bassuk & Rosenberg 1990]. Suggested techniques include freedom to change activities, a balance of quiet and active play, predominantly small groups, and individual activities with some occasional large group activities.

Field trips are also important parts of activity programs. Trips to fire stations, museums, and parks, and walks around the neighborhood give children new experiences. Photographs and experience stories dictated by children about these trips can be combined with books in the book corner or kept in language experience activity boxes. If there is enough room and a quiet place in the shelter, children and adults alike will welcome visits from local storytellers; artists and artisans; and other community figures, such as police officers and firefighters (taking into account the fear and suspicion many residents might harbor about the police).

Finally, whenever possible, cooking activities can be integral parts of activity programs. If there is no kitchen, an electric skillet will suffice. Cooking activities combine many needed skills: sensory experiences, math, following directions, learning to wait, and working together. In addition to the fun of eating the products, families can help with children's cooking experiences, eat with them, and clean up together.

Although the passage of the Stewart B. McKinney Homeless Assistance Act allows children to attend their former or local schools with free transportation provided, many school-age children in shelters do not attend school regularly—some not at all. Forty-three percent of the school-age homeless children in one study did not attend school [Hall & Maza 1990]. In addition, most studies of homeless children report that they are likely to have repeated grades and even to have fallen far behind their age-mates in low-income housing.

Whenever possible, school-age children should go to their former schools so they can keep their friends and have access to the special services that schools provide. If this is not possible, school-age children need individualized programs so they will be as close to their grade levels as possible when their families can move into more permanent housing. In addition to working on school skills, staff members should provide appropriate play activities to help further children's social, emotional, physical, and creative development.

An annotated bibliography of basic early childhood materials, published general sources of activities for preschool and school-age children, and several resources specifically designed for children in shelters appears at the end of this book. Just as with all programs, select activities from many sources to fit the needs of the children being served. I recommend a variety of open-ended materials and activities, since the children will be changing frequently and be of various ages and abilities.

Putting It All Together

Planning activity programs for children in shelters requires flexibility and creativity, as well as a knowledge of child development and family support. Selecting materials and activities that promote feelings of security, acceptance, and success is of primary importance. Even the most basic practicalities, such as scheduling appropriate spaces and adjusting hours of operation to meet the needs of children, may require considerable adaptation to fit into the overall programs of shelters.

Despite the stresses and pressures of shelter life, children in shelters are more alike than different from age-mates who live in their own homes. Activities that are beneficial and pleasurable for children in preschool and child care programs should work well in settings serving children in shelters.

References

Bassuk, E.L., & Rosenberg, L. (1990). Psychosocial characteristics of homeless children and children with homes. *Pediatrics, 85,* 257–261.

Bassuk, E.L., & Rubin, L. (1987). Homeless children: A neglected population. *American Journal of Orthopsychiatry, 57,* 279–286.

Gewirtzman, R., & Fodor, I. (1987). The homeless child at school: From welfare hotel to classroom. *Child Welfare, 66,* 237–245.

Gonzalez-Mena, J. (1990). *Infant/toddler caregiving: A guide to routines.* Sacramento: California Department of Education.

Grant, R. (1991). The special needs of homeless children: Early intervention at a welfare hotel. *Topics in Early Childhood Special Education,* 10(4): 76–91.

Hall, J.A., & Maza, P.L. (1990). No fixed address: The effects of homelessness on families and children in N.A. Boxill (Ed.), *Homeless children: The watchers and the waiters.* Binghamton, NY: The Haworth Press.

Koblinsky, S.A., & Anderson, E.G. (1993). Serving homeless children and families in Head Start. *Children Today, 22*(3), 19–23, 36.

Molnar, J., with Klein, T., Knitzer, J., and Ortiz-Torres, B. (1988). *Home is where the heart is: The crisis of homeless children and families in New York City.* New York: Bank Street College of Education.

Further Reading

Brown, J.F. (Ed.). (1983). *Curriculum planning for young children.* Washington, DC: National Association for the Education of Young Children.

Cataldo, C.Z. (1983). *Infants and toddler programs: A guide to very early childhood education.* Menlo Park, CA: Addison-Wesley Publishing Company.

Garbarino, J. (1992). *Children in danger: Coping with the consequences of community violence.* San Francisco: Jossey-Bass Publishers.

Jenks, C. (1994). *The homeless.* Cambridge, MA: Harvard University Press.

Klein, T., Bittel, C., & Molnar, J. (1993). No place to call home: Supporting the needs of homeless children in the early childhood classroom. *Young Children, 48*(6), 22–31.

Koralek, D.G., Colker, L. J., & Dodge, D.T. (1993). *The what, why, and how of high-quality early childhood education: A guide for on-site supervision.* Washington, DC: National Association for the Education of Young Children.

McCormick, L., & Holden, R. (1992). Homeless children: A special challenge. *Young Children, 47*(6), 61–67.

Robertson, J.M., & Greenblatt, M. (Eds.). (1992). *Homelessness: A national perspective.* New York: Plenum Press.

Stronge, J.H. (Ed.). (1992). *Educating homeless children and adolescents: Evaluating policy and practice.* New York: Plenum Press.

Stronge, J.H., & Tenhouse, C. (1990). *Educating homeless children: Issues and answers.* Bloomington, IN: Phi Delta Kappa Educational Foundation.

Walsh, M.E. (1992). *"Moving to nowhere": Children's stories of homelessness.* Westport, CT: Auburn House.

Health Problems of Children in Shelters

Sandra Botstein & Pam Rolandelli

Medical professionals refer to a "homeless child syndrome," acknowledging the heightened vulnerability directly related to the social environment these children experience [American Academy of Pediatrics 1988]. Specific features of homelessness that impact children's physical well-being may include inadequate diet and locations for sleep, limited facilities for daily hygiene, exposure to the elements, communal sleeping and bathing facilities, and extreme poverty [Wright 1990]. The close and frequent contact among families within shelters presents optimum conditions for transmitting infectious diseases. The potential for spreading illnesses is further increased by the constant population turnover within shelters. Yet few shelters screen new residents for communicable diseases or make provisions for isolating those who are infected.

The physical health problems of children in shelters are basically the same as those of children living in their own homes. They include upper respiratory infections, ear disorders, gastrointestinal problems, and minor skin ailments; but the rate of occurrence among homeless children is much higher. Upper respiratory and ear infections occur twice as often; skin ailments and gastrointestinal problems, four times as often. Chronic physical disorders, such as anemia, cardiac disease, and neurological disorders are also found nearly twice as often among homeless children [Wright 1990].

In one New York City study, homeless children were found to have higher concentrations of lead in their blood than children of similar socioeconomic status living at home [Alperstein et al. 1988]. The full effects of low-level lead poisoning may not be immediately obvious, but the poisoning can contribute to serious behavioral and learning problems.

Problems with development and psychological functioning have also been reported in studies of children living in shelters for homeless people and shelters for victims of domestic violence. Nearly half of the homeless children in a Boston study had at least one developmental delay, one-third demonstrated severe depression and anxiety, and nearly half required formal psychiatric evaluation [Bassuk & Rubin 1987]. In another study, children living in domestic violence shelters experienced more psychological distress, reflected in withdrawn and aggressive behavior, than did other children [Hughes 1986]. And problems with mood, sleep, health, and social interaction were evident in yet another survey of over 900 children [Layzer et al. 1986].

Children residing in shelters often lack the basic pediatric care that can prevent many illnesses. One study found that immunizations and tuberculosis testing were substantially missing in homeless children in New York City [Alperstein et al. 1988]. Over half of the children in a Washington State study had no regular health provider; 35% did not have insurance coverage [Miller & Liro 1988].

Although the critical need for basic medical care for this population is widely recognized, access to health care systems is sorely lacking. As a result, homeless people's use of emergency room services is three times higher than that of the general population. Even where clinics do exist, parents may not take advantage of their services because they are preoccupied with finding homes, jobs, or food for their families. When parents do seek help for ill children, they must overcome a maze of obstacles, such as finding transportation, arriving within limited hours, waiting in long lines, and coping with sometimes confusing paperwork.

An additional problem is that some parents are not able to carry out prescribed treatments for their children. Once children have seen physicians, parents living in shelters sometimes fail to comply with recommended treatments because they do not understand the instructions, they have difficulty with proper storage of medication, or they have to administer medication at inconvenient times. As a result, health problem often recur.

It is apparent, therefore, that children living in shelters suffer physical illnesses more frequently than their domiciled counterparts and are limited in their access to basic health care. The challenge of providing adequate health care for children in shelters calls for attention in both shelters and communities. Shelters must establish policies and practices that reduce the incidence of infectious diseases and improve access to community health resources. Safety precautions are also necessary to prevent accidents and injuries. Communities should develop accessible health care for families and children in shelters—this chapter ends with a description of an innovative program to illustrate one community's approach.

Health Provisions in Shelters

Shelters should screen families for current illnesses when they are admitted and provide isolation areas for people who are ill to reduce the spread of infections. Shelters should ask for health information on intake forms, such as recent illnesses, children's immunizations, and health records. Shelters should arrange for periodic visits by nurses or pediatricians to advise them on their health practices and to offer basic health care to resident children. Shelters should develop health and hygiene policies for staff members and residents and ensure that everyone is informed about the policies upon entry and periodically thereafter. Shelters should also designate health back-ups for after-hours calls and develop emergency plans.

Suggested Practices

Hand washing

- Encourage residents and staff members to wash hands regularly, especially upon arrival; before preparing, serving, or eating food; after using toilets; and after changing diapers or helping children with toileting. Faucets retain germs from dirty hands, so ask residents and staff members to use paper towels to turn off faucets to reduce the spread of germs. Put reminders in highly visible places in bathrooms and kitchens.

- Provide liquid soap and disposable paper towels near sinks for hand washing.

- Encourage children to wash their hands, especially upon arrival, after using the toilet or being diapered, and before and after eating.

Diapering

- Provide designated, convenient places for changing diapers near sinks but separated from food preparation areas. Have all supplies available for residents to keep diapering areas clean and sanitary. If this is not possible, diapers should be changed only in children's own cribs. Sheets, bedding, and cribs should be cleaned and disinfected before being used by other children.

- Encourage residents to use sanitary diapering procedures, which can reduce children's chances of contracting diarrhea and other gastrointestinal illnesses:

- Put fresh paper on changing tables before laying babies down.

- Dispose of dirty diapers and soiled wipes in lined, covered trash cans.

- Throw used paper in trash cans.

- Clean with soap and water, if necessary, and sanitize the tops of changing tables with bleach solution.

- When finished, parents should wash their own hands and their children's hands thoroughly.

- Turn off faucets with paper towels after washing hands.

Protection from HIV infection

There have been no reported cases of transmitting the human immunodeficiency virus (HIV) from one person to another in out-of-home child care, but no current data directly address this question [APHA & AAP 1992].

Although HIV has been found in saliva and urine in very low volumes, studies have shown that people infected with HIV do not spread the virus to other members of their households by sharing toothbrushes, washcloths, or drinking glasses. HIV is spread by sexual contact with an infected person; exchange of needles or syringes used by an infected person; pregnancy, birth, or breast-feeding if the mother is infected; or transfusions of infected blood, blood products, or organ transplants [Taylor-Brown 1991]. In isolated cases, contact with blood from an infected person has been another possible mode of transmission.

Caregivers working with children in group care should follow universal precautions established by the Centers for Disease Control and Prevention (CDC) for handling blood and blood-containing fluids [APHA & AAPA 1992].

- All spills of blood or blood-containing body fluids should be cleaned and disinfected. CDC suggests a disinfectant solution of ¼ cup of household liquid chlorine bleach added to 1 gallon of tap water, prepared fresh daily. A slight chlorine odor indicates that the solution is still effective. If there is no chlorine smell, make a new solution, even if the solution was prepared fresh that day.

- Caregivers should wear nonporous gloves to clean these spills and should wash their hands after disposing of the gloves.

- Caregivers cleaning contaminated surfaces should avoid exposing open sores or mucous membranes to bloody spills.

- Mops should be cleaned, rinsed in sanitizing solutions, wrung as dry as possible, and hung up to dry completely.

- Blood-contaminated material and diapers should be disposed of in plastic bags with secure ties.

Children infected with HIV are at increased risk for severe complications from chicken pox, cytomegalovirus, tuberculosis, and measles. HIV-infected children exposed to chicken pox or measles should be referred immediately to health care providers. Caregivers known to be HIV-positive should be notified if they have been exposed to children with measles, chicken pox, or tuberculosis.[1]

Lead poisoning

Lead poisoning is most dangerous for pregnant women and children under age 6. It is not easily detected because symptoms, such as abdominal pains, muscular weakness, or fatigue, are often similar to those of flu or other illnesses. Undetected, lead poisoning can lower children's IQs, impair memory, and seriously affect their ability to concentrate.

Lead poisoning is caused by swallowing or breathing lead from a variety of sources.

- Lead-based paint dust from the renovation of older homes or peeling paint in and around older homes is one of the primary sources.

- Lead in drinking water usually comes from lead pipes and solder in home plumbing. Water that has not been used for six hours is likely to contain more lead than water from a tap used recently.

- Nearly all brands of miniblinds manufactured before 1996—but especially those manufactured overseas—use lead to stabilize their color. Exposure to sunlight causes the lead to break down, which then mixes with house dust on the blinds. Most retailers now sell miniblinds without lead.

- Dietary sources of lead include acidic foods stored in opened metal cans or foods from dented cans, which absorb lead from the solder in the cans.

- Printed paper, such as magazines, newspapers, and comics, often contain lead in their inks and can be harmful to children who chew on the paper. Burning printed paper, painted wood, or automobile battery casings can create lead dust or fumes.

---

[1] For further information, call the National AIDS Hotline, 800/342-AIDS (800/344-SIDA for Spanish-speaking callers), 24 hours a day, seven days a week.

Tips to Prevent Lead Poisoning

1. Cover cracked, flaking, or chewable painted surfaces with cloth or contact paper until the paint can be permanently removed or covered.

2. Remove or replace old miniblinds with new, lead-free blinds.

3. Sweep up paint flakes and wet-mop daily, using high-phosphate cleansers such as Spic-n-Span.

4. Wash your hands and children's hands frequently.

5. Don't allow children to eat paint, paper, or dirt or put dirty hands or toys in their mouths.

6. Store food in plastic, glass, or stainless steel containers, never in open metal cans.

7. Don't burn newspapers, painted boards, or battery casings.

8. Use lead-free interior paints on walls, furniture, and toys.

9. Check plumbing for lead solder or pipes. Have the water tested if you think it contains lead.

10. Allow water to run from the cold tap until it becomes noticeably cooler before using.

11. Never use hot tap water for drinking, cooking, or making baby formula.

Adapted from *The Hazards of Lead,* a pamphlet published by the Environmental Epidemiology Section, North Carolina Department of Environment, Health, and Natural Resources.

Since exposure to lead can have serious effects, all children ages 1 to 5 should be tested for lead. This involves a simple finger-stick blood test that can be performed at local health departments. A second blood test is recommended if a child's initial screening test shows that lead may be a problem.

Safety Measures

Accidents are the leading cause of death for preschoolers. There are no safety standards, however, or requirements for inspection of shelters that house children. Consequently, shelter environments may not be childproofed and may present many dangers for child residents.

The checklists in Appendix A provide guidelines for assessing the safety of shelter sites and playgrounds. The site safety checklist will help in childproofing shelters. It covers hazards that may be found in kitchens, bathrooms, and general environments and includes suggestions for preparing for emergencies. The playground safety checklist is a compilation of suggested guidelines based on Consumer Product Safety Commission guidelines, international playground standards, and expert opinions from consultants in the field of playground safety. Playground injuries may happen with many types of equipment and environmental conditions, but falls from climbing equipment account for a large portion of reported injuries. Using resilient surfacing materials under play equipment is therefore imperative. (See Chapter 3, "Creating Environments for Play.")[2]

Community Health Care Measures

Action on a community level is also necessary to provide needed services for children in shelters. Since every community's needs and resources are unique, local advocates must decide which of the following options will work best in their own communities.

- Invite local pediatricians and public health professionals to visit and learn about shelters and their residents. Encourage them to volunteer their time.

- Contact local hospitals to find out what free services and programs they can provide for children in shelters.

- Establish family health care provider teams, based in clinics, to visit shelters to deal with acute health problems.

- Establish mobile clinics to provide basic care to a number of shelters by visiting them on specific days.

- Establish neighborhood clinics near shelters or directly on site.

An Innovative Program: The New York Children's Health Project

The New York Children's Health Project (NYCHP) provides comprehensive pediatric care with extensive follow-up and outreach to homeless, housing-vulnerable, and indigent children living in New York City. To meet the complex and diverse needs of these children, the project has developed a multifaceted program that includes primary care pediatrics,

---

[2] For more information about health and safety in out-of-home child care, contact the National Resource Center for Health and Safety in Child Care, 2000 15th Street North, Suite 701, Arlington, VA 22301-2617; 703/524-7802.

outreach and follow-up, mental health services, child abuse identification and management, and adolescent medicine and substance abuse.

The idea for the program originated during a 1986 visit to a welfare hotel by singer-songwriter Paul Simon and Irwin Redlener, chief of ambulatory pediatrics at New York Hospital. The poverty, lack of nutritious food, and lack of basic medical care were overwhelming, and Simon organized a benefit concert to raise money to launch the project and donated $80,000 to buy the first van. Redlener persuaded New York Hospital to donate staffing and office space to the effort.

Two mobile medical units staffed by pediatricians, nurses, and nurse practitioners operate daily and regularly visit welfare hotels for homeless people; congregate care centers for foster children; and gathering places for runaway youths in Brooklyn, Manhattan, and Queens.

The medical units provide primary care, with a range of services, including routine well-child, preventive care; physical examinations; care for acute illnesses; follow-up care for chronic illnesses; and health education and counseling services. Fifty-five percent of the patients seen in 1989 were infants and preschool-age children. Approximately 65% of the visits were for the evaluation of acute or chronic illness. The rest of the visits were primarily for health maintenance assessments. A computerized medical record system aids the staff in providing continuing care for these transient populations. In addition, staff members work closely with appropriate support services and government agencies that serve the general needs of the children and their families.

The project has benefited from the support and involvement of the New York Hospital–Cornell University Medical Center. Patients using the mobile medical units are registered as New York Hospital patients and have immediate and full access to all of the institution's facilities and clinics. The problem of families missing follow-up treatments at the hospital has been overcome by having the hospital's transportation service pick up patients and return them home after their appointments.

Both private and public sources fund the project. Medicaid pays for most patient visits. A substantial part of the support comes from private foundations and contributors, and a grant from the U.S. Department of Housing and Urban Development, through the Stewart B. McKinney Homeless Assistance Act, partly funds the operating budget.

NYCHP is National Children's Health Demonstration Project. As such, it explores ways of creating the most effective models for the health care needs of disadvantaged children. Planners and providers from other cities are encouraged to contact the project to obtain information on its fiscal and operational systems.

The Children's Health Fund is a foundation developed to fund NYCHP activities and assist communities in developing innovative child health programs where access to care is limited. The foundation provides assistance through

- technical program development;
- fiscal planning, standardized data collection, and analysis systems;
- grants for acquiring mobile medical units; and
- start-up grants, with a maximum of $100,000 per year for up to three years.

Ultimately, the foundation hopes to create a national network of innovative child health care for highly disadvantaged populations.[3]

References

Alperstein, G., Rappaport, C., & Flanigan, J.M., (1988). Health problems of homeless children in New York City. *American Journal of Public Health, 78,* 1232–1233.

American Academy of Pediatrics, Committee on Community Health Services. (1988). Health needs of homeless children. *Pediatrics, 82,* 938–940.

American Public Health Association (APHA) & the American Academy of Pediatrics (AAP). (1992). *Caring for our children: National health and safety performance standards: Guidelines for out-of-home child care programs.* Washington, DC, and Elk Grove Village, IL: Authors

Bassuk, E., & Rubin, L. (1987). Homeless children: A Neglected population. *American Journal of Orthopsychiatry, 57,* 279–286.

Hughes, H. (1986, March/April). Research with children in shelters. *Children Today, 15,* 21–25.

Layzer, J.I., Goodsen, B.D., & deLange, C. (1986, March/April). Children in shelters. *Children Today, 15,* 6–11.

Miller, D.S., & Liro, E.H.V. (1988). Children in sheltered homeless families: Reported health status and use of health services. *Pediatrics, 81,* 668–673.

North Carolina Department of Environment, Health, and Natural Resources, Environmental Epidemiology Section. (n.d.). *The hazards of lead.* [Pamphlet]. Raleigh, NC: Author.

Taylor-Brown, S. (1991). AIDS: The reality in all our lives. *Family Resource Coalition Report, 10*(2), 12–13.

Wright, J.D. (1990). Homelessness is not healthy for children and other living things. In N. Boxill (Ed.), *Homeless children: The watchers and the waiters.* Binghamton, NY: The Haworth Press.

---

[3] Inquiries and applications should be directed to Karen Redlener, New York Children's Health Project/Children's Health Fund, 317 East 64th Street, New York, NY 10021; 212/535-9400.

Support and Education Programs for Parents

Tovah Klein and Mary Foster

The profile of most families living in shelters nationally is a female single parent with two to three children [Bassuk et al. 1986]. These parents often are young. Many have less than a high-school education. A study of homeless families in New York City found that poverty and economic stress take a heavy toll on parents' mental health [Molnar et al. 1991]. Nearly half of the parents in the study had reported levels of depression that warranted referrals for treatment. Findings suggested a relation between parents' levels of symptoms of depression and children's problem behaviors. These results further emphasize the importance of addressing the needs of parents to support the welfare of the children.

For many families, entering a shelter is one in a series of moves or recent traumas. Parents in shelters are under stress. They may be unable to cope with their children's basic needs and with the other demands that homelessness places on families. Shelters may have to provide respite care for young children either on site or in other facilities. Respite alone, however, is not enough. Parents also need advocates who can help them become more self-sufficient. Advocates can help ensure that individual and group support programs are offered.

Parent Educators and Support Staff

A key ingredient of success for parent support programs in shelters is having at least one person who provides informal, caring support for both parents and children throughout their stays. Such a person is available to talk with parents over coffee in the morning, to play with children during the day, to help parents talk with their children about feelings, or to manage children's difficult behaviors as they occur. Usually, parent educators carry out this function.

The Role of Parent Educators

- Parent educators provide relevant information and offer support and other resources for parents.

- Parent educators are sensitive and empathic listeners with excellent problem-solving skills.

- Parent educators have solid backgrounds in child development and children's responses to trauma, and they are able to help parents build effective coping skills.

- Parent educators provide positive models of effective parenting, demonstrating nonpunitive methods of discipline and warm, supportive interactions.

- Parent educators understand their professional limits and how the role of family support differs from that of therapists. Parents who bring up problems of substance abuse or childhood sexual or physical abuse, who appear to be clinically depressed, or who present other mental health problems should be referred to appropriate services for help.

Responsibilities of Parent Educators

- Parent educators build bonds of mutual trust and respect with parents. Trust can be developed through one-on-one sessions, parent support groups, and daily contact. The most meaningful interactions often take place informally around kitchen tables.

- Parent educators empower parents to take control over their own lives and their children's lives by involving them in planning for their children.

- Parent educators help parents and children understand the grief they may be experiencing.

- Parent educators help parents understand the importance of stability in their children's lives and work with them on ways to establish routines for their children.

- Parent educators help parents develop realistic expectations for their children's behavior, based on an understanding of developmental stages, to guide them effectively.

- Parent educators strengthen parent-child bonds that may have undergone serious disruption and have to be restored.

Informal Approaches to Parent Education

Individualized parent education begins with a brief interview at the time of intake, when only emergency medical information, current medication and known allergies, the names of children's legal guardians, and children's dates of birth have to be obtained. Shelters' child-related policies should be mentioned at intake as well. Most shelters have policies against physical punishment, which should be explained to parents. Give parents a list of disciplinary alternatives, and urge them to seek help from staff members if they encounter problems.

Within two or three days of families' admission to shelters, parent educators can request individual meetings with parents to determine their children's immediate needs. Parent educators should determine parents' receptivity to parenting programs at this time, expressing empathy with parents about the difficulty of their situations and letting them know they can turn to shelter staff members for support.

Regularly scheduled individual sessions are perhaps the most important and effective components of individualized parenting programs. Most parents feel that weekly sessions are sufficient, but some may prefer to meet more frequently. Individual meetings can cover parents' worries about themselves or their children. Maintaining nonjudgmental, respectful attitudes is of the utmost importance. Parent educators should emphasize

- recognition that parents know and want what is best for their children;
- recognition that the parents are doing the best they can for their children, given the limited resources available to them;
- helping parents articulate their goals for their children and themselves; and
- deciding together what actions parents undertake to achieve their goals.

Parents will often volunteer much information about their own and their children's backgrounds as they begin to trust and feel comfortable with parent educators. Often, these sessions can help shelter staff members to construct families' social histories. Parent educators should not tape-record sessions and should avoid taking notes; but if it does become necessary, they should explain why they are taking notes and how the notes will be used.

Invite all parents to weekly informal coffee hours. Snacks at these meetings contribute to a relaxed, nurturing, and open atmosphere to which parents respond. During these unstructured gatherings, facilitators can assess parents' needs informally and plan topics for future sessions. Discipline is the most frequently requested topic. Hands-on presentations that provide real-life experiences, such as role-playing, are most effective, as are brainstorming about effective problem-solving approaches.

Formal Approaches to Parent Education

Because most families live in shelters only temporarily, completing more structured, long-term parent education programs may not be possible. Sections of commercial programs, however, such as Parent Effectiveness Training, may be included as part of individual sessions or support groups, even if there is insufficient time to complete the entire series. Select only those portions of such programs that are relevant to the parents in the group. When formal programs have been selected, group facilitators should be certified instructors, and text-books and workbooks should be provided free to participants. Perhaps the best way to apply these commercial programs is to use tapes and workbooks to facilitate discussions, which can continue more informally. Some parents may not be receptive to structured programs, and attendance at these workshops should not be mandatory. Several parent education programs may be useful:

- **Parent Effectiveness Training** teaches concrete skills and practical procedures that help parents rear their children [Gordon 1970]. It is a comprehensive program aimed at establishing and maintaining effective parent-child relationships. Through descriptions and case studies, the program covers principles of effective parenting, techniques for keeping channels of communication open, using appropriate discipline, and resolving parent-child conflicts. The program's goal is to help parents rear responsible, self-disciplined, co-operative children.

- *Raising America's Children* is a 10-part, half-hour public television series that provides child development information for parents and professionals, including family child care providers, child care center staff members, and preschool and kindergarten teachers [Harms & Cryer 1990]. The program describes practical ways to improve the quality of life for children from birth to age 6 and how to ensure children's emotional, physical, and intellectual well-being. Instructors' guides and viewer study guides are available.

Issues Affecting Parenting Programs in Shelters

Mistrust of service providers can be a major issue for many families. Parents often have been in contact with numerous service providers before entering shelters. These agencies likely have asked many questions that the parents felt were intrusive, attacking, or too personal. As a result, parents may appear apprehensive when asked questions about their family situations. Staff members should be especially sensitive to this problem, asking only for information that is absolutely necessary.

Staff members should also be aware of how their own actions may usurp or weaken parents' roles. Parent-child relationships strongly influence children's health, growth, and development. The lack of privacy in shelters makes it difficult for parents to build and maintain these relationships. Family interactions are open to public scrutiny and, at times, public intervention. Researchers studying women and children staying at a night shelter observed what they termed the unraveling of the parents' roles resulting from being deprived of control over routines, rules, and setting standards for their children [Boxill & Beaty 1990]. Giving parents opportunities to make decisions about their children and providing time and space for privacy will foster stronger relationships between parents and children.

Providing parent involvement and education programs in shelters is a challenging task. A combination of approaches and the willingness to learn, improvise, and change are necessary ingredients in implementing successful programs. Helping parents help themselves and feel successful in their roles as parents can benefit them and their children immensely. The more confident parents become, the better they are able to nurture and guide their children.

Involving Parents in Early Childhood Programs

Just as children can benefit from parent-focused programs, parents can benefit from child-focused programs. An increasing number of early childhood programs are serving homeless children, off-site as well as in shelters, including preschools, Head Start, and part- or full-time care. These programs provide opportunities to develop effective approaches for meeting the needs of parents. To help staff members overcome the initial mistrust that parents may feel, programs should solicit parental participation gently, without being demanding or intrusive. Shelter residents are already overwhelmed; children's programs should not add more stress. Rather, staff members should be encouraging and supportive, with the goal of building trust first and increasing parental involvement gradually over time.

How can programs accomplish such goals while providing services for parents who are ready to participate? First, programs must be flexible to meet the widely differing needs of parents and the variability in their willingness to participate. This flexibility can be frustrating to staff members who observe some parents' lack of parenting skills and who want to require parent training immediately. Although being good caregivers and child advocates is important, so too is recognizing the vast unmet needs of the parents. Without attention to these needs, parents often cannot provide for their children. If the staff can help parents cope with their own needs, parents, in turn, will be able to provide better care for their children. Programs should therefore establish welcoming and supportive atmospheres and let parents decide whether to participate.

How Programs Can Support Parents

Provide parent rooms or spaces for parents

Many parents are young and in need of support and nurturing. Caring for their children is difficult when they do not feel nurtured themselves. Parent rooms are special places where parents can meet other parents informally to build peer support. The space can also be used for more structured activities. Parent rooms should be comfortable and inviting, with refreshments provided. It is easy for people to get to know each other over coffee without feeling the pressure of formal meetings. When setting up parent rooms, staff members may want to ask parents for help in deciding what to include. This promotes parents' sense of ownership and lets them feel like part of the project. Some suggestions for parents' rooms include:

Clothes-sharing areas. Many programs receive donations. Clothes-sharing areas allow shelters to display donated clothes and let parents select what they want for themselves and their children. Rather than being given clothes, parents can decide what they need and like. This lets them make decisions about their children. In many other domains, their decision-making authority has been taken away. Early childhood programs can provide ways for parents to make decisions regarding their children, thus supporting them in their roles as parents and helping them regain confidence in their parenting abilities.

Book- and toy-sharing areas. Donated books and toys can be displayed, and parents can choose items for their children. Again, this allows parents to decide what they want or need.

Hands-on activities can including crafts, cooking, sewing, holiday activities, or toy making. Try to include parents in selecting activities, and organize activities that parents and children can do together, such as cooking or making art dough. Such activities foster parent-child relationships and allow staff members to model effective parenting skills.

Literature and information. Provide handouts for parents on a range of topics, including birth control, nutrition, parenting, drugs, and other topics of interest. This information may complement topics discussed in support groups. Information should be available in languages other than English, if necessary, to accommodate parents' needs.

Organize parent activities

Help parents connect. Parents can support each other in many ways, and the program can facilitate their meeting other parents and building friendships through shared activities. Parent rooms provide ideal settings for parents to meet informally over coffee, for making art projects, or for taking general educational development classes. Encourage parents to plan activities together for their children; this helps them build support networks.

Arrange outings for the parents. They are under great stress and need time to relax and enjoy themselves. Outings can include movies, a sports day, or going out for lunch or a picnic. By arranging fun activities for parents, shelters convey the message that their programs are there to help parents, not just children. As staff members help parents feel special, parents can better nurture their children.

Support groups, led by professionals, can help parents deal with matters that concern them. Early childhood program staff members should coordinate with the parent educators or family-child advocates at their shelters to avoid duplicating services. When forming groups, encourage parents to decide what topics they want to discuss. Although staff members may have ideas about what should be covered, parents may not want to focus on their children when they have their own problems. By letting parents choose, staff members empower parents to decide what is important for them, instead of being told what they should do. Parents often select topics focusing on personal problems of loss or abuse. Groups dealing with discipline, parenting skills, and stress can help parents find ways to handle parenting more effectively.

Help parents understand and appreciate their children and realize that they are important to their children

Many parents feel that their children do not care whether they are around. Telling them, "Your child misses you," may be a new insight for parents who have not learned to feel special and needed. They learn that other adults are not replacements for them. This can strengthen the connection between parents and their children. Making sure parents say good-bye to their children when they leave further reinforces feelings of importance and makes separations easier.

Facilitate connections between parents and children. Provide frequent reports about what children are doing. Emphasize positive experiences and achievements, and let parents know how wonderful their children's growth is. For example, "Antonio built a house out of blocks today with Brad. He's really learning how to share and cooperate." This helps parents feel good about their children and informs them about their children's development. Programs may want to send weekly newsletters reporting what groups did during the week, and attach brief personal notes for each child. Newsletters can include activities as well as songs or finger plays that the children know well, so the parents can do these activities with their children.

Send home artwork. Let children take their artwork with them and, if possible, let children mount their artwork for display in shelters. Be sure to provide tape with the artwork, since many parents in shelters will not have such extras. Again, this helps parents better understand and appreciate their children and delight in their growth and accomplishments.

Take photographs of the children. Photographs are nice ways to help parents connect. Send parents pictures of their children engaged in various activities. The photos often act as springboards for children to tell their parents what they did at school. All parents enjoy having photos of their children. When families enroll, take their pictures to hang in the child care room. This helps children with separation and reminds parents that they are important parts of their children's lives. When children leave shelters, they can take the photos with them in albums or notebooks.

Remember special occasions. Help children remember parents on special occasions, including birthdays and holidays. Children can make cards and gifts that bring great delight to parents and make them feel special. Cards or gifts that children make themselves are preferable.

Involve parents in decisions regarding their child. Ask parents about their children's developmental histories, temperaments, likes and dislikes. This can be done in formal meetings with parents when children are enrolled, as well as informally at drop-off and pick-up times. If decisions are to be made regarding children's programs or special services, make sure parents are involved in decision making. Respect their ideas and concerns. Ultimately, parents know their children best.

Enable parents to give to their children. Programs can enable parents to maintain their parenting roles and provide for their children during times when they may not be able to do so financially. For example, during Christmas or other holidays, staff members can provide materials and opportunities for parents to give gifts to their children. If toys have been donated, allow parents to choose gifts to give to their children. If shelters have money for presents, they can let parents suggest what they want to give their children. Provide materials so that parents can wrap the presents and make cards. This allows them to provide holiday celebrations for their children. Consult with parents about possible alternatives and ways in which they can participate more actively.

Let parents have birthday parties for their children at the shelter. Shelter staff members can provide some items, and the parents can bring others. Again, parents give parties for their children with the help of shelter staff, not vice versa.

Educate parents about child development. Many parents do not know what is developmentally appropriate or how learning takes place. It is important to help them understand how children learn and develop. This can help them become informed consumers of educational programs. There are many ways to help parents learn about growth and development.

Have parents' nights at your programs

Provide child care while parents are invited to participate in their children's activities, from painting and art dough to puzzles, stories, and blocks. Many parents never have had opportunities to see early childhood programs, so they do not understand the importance of such programs for their children's development. By participating in activities, parents gain understanding of how children learn through play. Teachers can demonstrate this for parents. For example, they can lead parents in putting together large puzzles while talking about the use of language, counting, and working together.

Involve parents as classroom volunteers

Invite parents to help on field trips or to assist in classrooms. This gives teachers opportunities to act as role models for interacting in developmentally appropriate ways. Parents who are new to the shelter can feel overwhelmed if they must stay all day, however. Be flexible and allow parents to be involved in whatever capacity they feel comfortable. Parents should be able to just visit and enjoy watching their children. But if they are being relied upon to serve as part of the staff that day, their duties must be spelled out very carefully, since the health and safety of all the children are involved.

Organization is one key to good parent participation. Physical facilities should be easy to understand, with many visual cues such as pictures or labels so that parents can see where things belong. If there are rules for how or where things are to be used, parents must know that, too. Schedules should be posted for all adults to see, and clocks should be available so that everyone operates within the same time frames.

Staff members may want to limit the number of parents in classrooms to one or two at a time. Have activities ready for them in advance. Parents should feel comfortable and competent, yet supported. Staff members must take responsibility to oversee activities and intervene if conflicts or discipline problems arise.

Parent-cooperative preschools have learned many ways to guide and support parents as classroom volunteers. Many use laminated parent job cards that can be pinned upside down at waist height for easy reference. Job cards not only remind parents about what to do, but also signal children that their parents are helpers. Staff members can prepare several different types of job cards—story-reading cards, art cards, or music cards, for example. Parents can choose the jobs with which they feel most comfortable. Job card instructions should be brief and clear, including such basics as where to get materials and where to return them, directions for conducting activities, helpful hints for getting children involved, and when to clean up.

Provide concrete, supportive services for parents

Parents who are homeless or in severe crisis require levels of service that greatly exceed the parent support activities in most early childhood programs. If your program is not located in a shelter, it is best to contact the shelters served by your program to find out the types of assistance they provide for parents, such as referrals for medical care, substance abuse counseling, educational or vocational training, public assistance, housing, and the legal system. Work with shelters to help parents deal with the areas that cause stress and difficulties in their lives.

Supporting Parents

The goal of support and education programs directed toward parents in shelters is to help them gain, or perhaps regain, self-sufficiency and positive feelings about themselves. Parents can obtain support in coping with their own problems through trusting and helpful relationships with shelter and early childhood program staff. Parents should not feel burdened by the demands of parent support programs; rather, they should feel comfortable enough to decide on the levels of involvement they can handle. To encourage involvement, staff members should be supportive and available while respecting parents' needs for space and respite. For parents who need respite from their children, the time away can help them cope. As parents feel able, their involvement in their children's programs educates them about their children's abilities and about child development in general. Through parent support and education programs, parents can learn to deal with their own difficulties, to feel competent and effective as parents, and gain better understandings of their children.

References

Bassuk, E.L., Rubin, L., & Lauriat, A.S. (1986). Characteristics of sheltered homeless families. *American Journal of Public Health, 76,* 1097–1101.

Boxill, N.A., & Beaty, A.L. (1990). Mother/child interaction among homeless women and their children in a public night shelter in Atlanta, Georgia. In Boxhill, N.A. (Ed.) *Homeless children: The watchers and the waiters* (pp. 49–64). Binghamton, NY: The Haworth Press.

Gordon, T. (1970). *Parent effectiveness training.* New York: P.H. Wyden.

Harms, T., & Cryer, D., in cooperation with the University of North Carolina at Chapel Hill, Center for Public Television. (1990). *Raising America's children.* [Video]. Video and training materials available through Delmar Publishers, Albany, NY.

Molnar, J., Rath, W.R., Klein, T.P., Lowe, C., & Hartmann, A.H. (1991). *Ill fares the land: The consequences of homelessness and chronic poverty for children and families in New York City.* New York: Bank Street College of Education.

CHAPTER 8

Volunteers in Programs for Homeless Children

Pat Ward

Volunteers are increasingly important and visible components of advocacy, service delivery, and education efforts in the United States. Shelter programs, like other social services, can be improved and made more efficient by involving volunteers. This chapter clarifies what voluntarism is about; what we know about volunteers in shelter programs; how to recruit, train, and supervise volunteers; what is involved in evaluating volunteer programs; and what resources are available for planning to use volunteers effectively in local shelter child care programs. Appendixes B–F at the end of this book illustrate how others have recruited, trained, and supervised volunteers or have come to understand the context of volunteering in shelter programs.[1] The appendixes contain several forms, including a job description, communication tips, and discipline guidelines from exemplary shelter programs, as well as an annotated list of organizations that have helpful information on volunteers.

Although this chapter is intended to be practical with respect to theories, strategies, and tactics of using volunteers, it is not a procedural guide for developing a program. Rather, it provides a general basis from which the specifics of local thinking, planning, and implementation can evolve. The information on shelter programs and volunteers is based on a series of structured interviews with a small sample of homeless shelters with child care programs that use volunteers. The general ideas about voluntarism reflect the experiences of the National Council of Jewish Women (NCJW) as a volunteer organization. With 100,000 members nationwide, NCJW has a century-long history of services to children and families of all socioeconomic, ethnic, and religious backgrounds. NCJW also uses its volunteers'

[1] The author would like to thank Gabriel M. Della-Piana, Department of Educational Psychology, University of Utah, Salt Lake City, for his valuable comments on this chapter.

resources and expertise to build the capacity of existing organizations and to help emerging organizations and programs work on behalf of children and their families. Since 1911, NCJW has worked for universal high-quality child care. Local NCJW chapters, or sections, have initiated hundreds of community service, education, and advocacy projects toward this goal. NCJW sections are currently engaged in over 40 different projects to support homeless and domestic-violence shelter programs, many of which involve child care components.

Voluntarism Today

Most people are acquainted with volunteering since it is a part of the lives of so many people in the United States. Dramatic changes are taking place today, however, regarding who volunteers are, the types of activities in which they engage, and the amount of time they have available for those activities. A number of researchers have tried to characterize the personalities and motivations of volunteers [Bellah 1996, Van Til 1988, Abdennur 1987]. A discussion of these characterizations is beyond the scope of this chapter, but NCJW has made some interesting observations about voluntarism in the course of recent experiences [NCJW 1989].

Over the last 20 years, the rapid growth in the number of employed women has changed the nature of voluntarism. Increasingly, people who volunteer are doing so in addition to full- or part-time employment. The type of volunteer commitments that employed people are able to make are different than those of full-time volunteers. Employed people volunteer for fewer hours and are likely to choose volunteer work that is time-limited and can fit around their work schedules. Programs and organizations that use volunteers, therefore, have to be creative and flexible in designing roles, tasks, and schedules for volunteers. For example, goal-oriented, short-term projects may be more appealing to volunteers with full-time jobs [Mergenhagen 1991].

For volunteer positions that are less finite and involve ongoing responsibilities, other types of volunteers may nevertheless still be available. A small but significant number of people—especially women—still choose to volunteer full time. Devoting their energies to full-time volunteering enables them to become experts on the problems and services to which they are deeply committed.

In addition to employed people and full-time volunteers, youth and the elderly are growing presences in voluntarism. Students, for example, can be among the best volunteers. Often, they are highly motivated to succeed in their assignments, have definite periods of service, and are reliable in their attendance.

Shelter Child Care Programs and Volunteers

Volunteer Philosophy: Focus on Children's Needs

Child care programs for homeless children serve several purposes. Some are enrichment and intervention programs focused on children. Shelter child care programs can also be used to care for children while their parents are in skill-building workshops, 12-step programs, or parenting classes, or on the many appointments that homeless families make to obtain permanent housing, food, medical care, and other necessary services.

In child care programs for homeless children, the fundamental guiding principle should be that the adults who interact with the children help create consistent, trust-enhancing, predictable environments. Most people who volunteer in homeless children's programs do so because they want to make a difference in children's lives. No one questions the good intentions of volunteers, but programs that use them must resolve a few key issues. For example, children's needs should not take a back seat to the fiscal realities of child care programs and the desires of volunteers to spend their time in ways they see as valuable. Program staff members and volunteers must recognize the tensions caused by the competing factors of funding needs that necessitate the use of volunteers to supplement staff, the needs of volunteers who want to work with children, and children's needs for stability in their unpredictable worlds.

In the course of meeting children's needs, volunteers should be sensitive also to the necessity of strengthening parent-child relationships within families in the program. Volunteers should support parents and empower them to do things for their children. For example, many volunteer groups hold birthday and holiday parties for children in shelter programs and make opportunities available for parents to be involved in planning these parties. Parents choose gifts for their children and wrap and decorate packages. Sometimes parents help prepare party snacks and games. Afterward, parents feel proud that they had important roles in making the parties successful and in doing something special for their children. Another example of volunteers empowering parents involves a storyteller whose stories inspired some of the mothers in a shelter to learn storytelling, which resulted in the mothers improving their own literacy.

Who Volunteers?

In child care programs for homeless children, the greatest number of volunteers are involved in direct service. These hands-on volunteers are representative of traditional volunteers. They are mostly middle-class, middle-aged, Caucasian women between 40 and 60 years of age. More diversity occurs in volunteer activities that are not specific to child care. People from a wider range of age groups, income levels, and ethnicities, as well as a significant proportion of men, volunteer in a variety of other capacities. See Appendix B for the full range of possible volunteer roles in shelter programs.

In the child care programs interviewed, volunteers ranged in age from school-age to 80 years. For the most part, younger volunteers tend to be college students; middle-aged volunteers come from service organizations and clubs; and older volunteers are retired. When children younger than age 16—such as Girl Scouts or Future Teachers—volunteer with children, they always have adult group leaders with them.

Why Use Volunteers?

Shelter child care programs or any community service organizations use volunteers for many reasons. Volunteers can supplement, complement, and enrich administration and staff efforts in several ways. For instance:

- Volunteers can give children the individual attention and extra care that are crucial for some who are caught up in anger, fear, and a sense of loss. New children unaccustomed to being part of a group may need one-on-one attention to make the move into a group setting.

- Volunteers offer opportunities to children for positive interaction with people of all ages and genders. For example, because some children have abusive males in their lives, or live in shelters that may not allow entire families to live together, they can benefit from interaction with warm and caring male volunteers.

- Volunteers can develop special relationships with parents, who see that volunteers are there because they want to be and not because it is their job.

- Volunteer organizations can contribute financial and personal resources. Many shelters have been started through volunteer efforts.

- Volunteers have positive impacts on communities' self-images as caring. For example, volunteers can communicate the message that shelter programs are not ends in themselves but are in positions to illuminate the problems of homelessness and what has contributed to its existence.

- Skilled professionals who volunteer can perform legal work, fundraising, accounting, research, and communications functions.

For shelter child care programs to derive full benefit from their volunteers, staff members must remember certain points. Children experience constant change when their families are homeless, so the rotation and changing faces of volunteers may do more harm than good. Volunteers must be as regular and reliable as staff members, no matter how formal or informal the settings. For example, since many children are in shelter programs for limited periods, volunteers who tell them, "I'll see you next month," can undercut children's trust if they are no longer going to be in the program when the volunteers come again. No caring person intentionally wants to add to the already alarming array of people that pop in and out of homeless children's lives. Volunteers who work directly with children, therefore, have to commit enough time and energy to be consistent parts of shelter child care settings.

Using the talents of volunteers and simultaneously building children's trust, all in a very short time, is the challenge for programs. This consistency can be especially important during the Christmas holiday season, when a large number of people often choose to do volunteer work. A program blessed with a large influx of volunteers has to coordinate the number, presence, and activities of these volunteers carefully to ensure that the children in the program do not suffer additional disruptions and confusion during the holiday season. Consistency is also essential for volunteers who work with children in the classroom.

For some volunteer roles in shelter programs, however, consistency is not as important. Thus, one way to deal with the potential problem of changing volunteer faces is to encourage volunteers who are unable to make extensive time commitments to get involved in behind-the-scenes work and leadership roles, such as serving on boards and committees. The value of these roles may have to be explained to volunteers, staff members, funders, board members, and other community partners, especially if the popular notion of volunteering is direct service work.

Getting the Most from Volunteers

Recruiting Volunteers

What techniques can help shelter programs attract and use volunteers to improve the services they provide? Although volunteers participate in shelter programs in a variety of ways, the focus here is on volunteers working directly with children.[2] Volunteers can get involved in programs in several ways:

- Volunteer organizations often make their capabilities and volunteers available to programs working in locations in which they are particularly interested. NCJW, the Junior League, the League of Women Voters, Kiwanis International, and other service organizations such as churches and synagogues can be especially valuable partners both in developing and implementing programs using volunteers.

- Shelter programs may refer some volunteers whose interests they cannot match to other programs with similar services that may be more compatible. For example, programs that use daytime volunteers may refer those who are available only on evenings and weekends to other programs that can accommodate their schedules.

- Volunteers interested in particular kinds of problems or services may find suitable programs or organizations through the media or by word of mouth.

- Employer-supported volunteer initiatives encourage individual employees and employee service clubs to become involved in community improvement and philanthropic activities.

- Universities, colleges, and high schools with social work, child care, and related majors, or those offering service internships, often have students who volunteer in community programs to fulfill course requirements.

- Community referral programs can match interested individuals to programs or organizations looking for volunteers, and vice versa. These volunteer clearinghouses are most common in larger communities.

Recruitment is a process with a number of steps by which both programs and volunteer applicants determine whether volunteer assignments in shelters will be good for both. Taking certain steps in the recruiting process can reduce the risks of poor placements of volunteers and of additional unpredictable changes in the lives of children in shelter programs.

Outreach. Many programs give presentations to corporations and service organizations as education and funding outreach efforts.

---

[2] For general information on using volunteers effectively in any kind of human service program, see Points of Light Foundation [1992].

Although these presentations may not be intended as recruitment initiatives, they can result in organizational commitments of volunteers. In communities where community service is part of college or high-school curricula, programs receive many placement requests. Some volunteers choose to work within shelter communities and find out about child care programs that way. The different sources of volunteers listed above may also be useful for outreach efforts.[3]

Written handbooks and guidelines. Programs should develop application forms, task descriptions, and written guidelines such as handbooks. Task definitions and descriptions should be in writing and should outline precisely volunteers' activities and responsibilities. Even in programs with limited orientation procedures and written materials, written guidelines for discipline are common. Appendixes C and D are examples of these such materials.

Registration. Registration forms can be sent to prospective volunteers before they are interviewed, or prospective volunteers can fill them out on site. Registration forms should ask for names, addresses, home and business phone numbers, places of employment or schools attended, birth dates, Social Security numbers, and by whom volunteers were referred. Special interests, skills, previous volunteer activities, and personal references are also needed. Students should give their advisors' names and number of volunteer hours necessary to complete their course requirements. Registration forms should also seek applicants' consent for police background checks. Applicants should be informed at this time of any health requirements, such as tuberculosis tests.

Interviewing. Interviews should be thorough enough to determine applicants' abilities to fill the positions. Interviewers should allow 45 to 60 minutes for first interviews. They should describe the volunteer work to applicants and explain the responsibilities involved. Interviewers should find out as much as possible about applicants' qualities, including their tolerance for people's differences; their ability to maintain nonjudgmental attitudes; their enthusiasm, flexibility, emotional stability, and warmth; and their sensitivity to children of all ages. Direct experience working with children may also be required. Interviewers should discuss with applicants their experiences with children, other volunteer work, and leisure interests, as well as their motivations for volunteering. Why did the volunteer chose this shelter? What are the volunteer's expectations of the position? What would make it a good experience? Finally, any required training should be mentioned during the first interview.

---

[3]   For additional information on recruiting volunteers, see MacBride [1982] (Chapter 4, especially) and OPRE [1990].

Interviewers should evaluate interviews immediately after they take place and decide whether individual applicants should be interviewed further. Whichever staff members will be the volunteers' immediate supervisors—children's program coordinators or child development specialists, for example—should conduct second interviews. Second interviews might begin with reviewing job descriptions and discussing job-specific questions, including posing problematic situations that might arise in the course of the volunteers' work.

Retention

Because children in shelters have to deal with chaotic and constantly shifting living situations, they need people around them on whom they can rely. Volunteers therefore must make significant time commitments to allow feelings of trust to develop with the children with whom they interact. Volunteers' lengths of service can range from participating in one-time special events to working with programs from their inception. Many volunteers, however, can make only time-limited commitments. For example, students usually are available for one term, 12 to 16 weeks; and service organizations and clubs usually contract for typical club years, nine months. Program administrators have to match volunteers' time commitments with appropriate responsibilities. Designated staff members should offer ongoing supervision and develop evaluation procedures with volunteers.

Volunteers must respect the needs of families in the programs in which they work; but volunteers themselves must be respected in turn, and their own agendas for volunteering must be acknowledged. For volunteers to feel that their time is being spent wisely, their particular skills and contacts have to be identified and used. Their responsibilities should encompass what they want to contribute. This applies equally to individual volunteers, to boards of directors, and to other community partners. Volunteers do not want to feel that they are just told what to do. The length of time they remain in their positions often depends on the satisfaction and opportunity for personal growth that they draw from volunteering. Staff members and parents should not think of volunteers as convenient baby-sitters but rather as valued staff members whose services are acknowledged and appreciated.

Training

A shelter's philosophy regarding children should be known and agreed upon by all those who come into contact with children in the shelter. All volunteers and staff members, therefore, should receive child development training as it relates to these children—including weekend and relief staff and senior aides who may not be official shelter volunteers but are under the aegis of other agencies. Everyone involved should be working toward the same goals, consistent with the shelter's philosophy. Effective, comprehensive training allows volunteers to feel confident as they begin their work with children. Facilities with large numbers of volunteers may find it convenient to schedule training programs three or four times a year. Smaller facilities may arrange monthly or ongoing individual sessions.

The first phase of training involves orientation to the program, including a statement of philosophy and goals, as well as a discussion of policies and procedures that directly affect volunteers. This phase should cover also a brief history and tour of the shelter and children's play environment.

The next phase should explore child development principles and their application to the children's program. Shelter programs find it particularly challenging to be developmentally appropriate. Families in shelters move on and change, so predicting groups of children that will be in shelters at given times can be difficult. This unpredictability means that volunteers, staff members, equipment, and toys should accommodate children of all ages. At the beginning of the child development segment of training, volunteers should receive some background information sensitizing them to the needs of children in shelters, including the following points:

- Some people and families are homeless due to personal crises, such as divorce, death, substance abuse, or mental or physical problems; but an increasing number of families are becoming homeless due to shortcomings in the economy and social service system—for such reasons as unemployment, low-wage jobs, inadequate low-income housing, and cuts in human service budgets. Most parents and homeless families can, with help, become self-supporting [CDF 1991].

- Some children in shelters come from traumatic family backgrounds involving alcohol or drug abuse, domestic violence, and child or spouse abuse. These children may display angry, acting-out behaviors, or may be withdrawn or developmentally delayed.

- The significant trauma that each of these children has experienced has to be confronted. The great losses they have experienced result in grieving, characterized in turn by anger, depression, and withdrawal, leaving them with reasons not to trust others.

Before new volunteers have any contact with shelter families or their records, they should sign confidentiality statements to protect the privacy of the children and their families. When volunteers complete their training, both volunteers and agencies should sign contractual agreements that cover volunteers' responsibilities to the agencies and agencies' responsibilities to volunteers.

Volunteers can receive experiential training in child development by playing with children and describing and discussing what happened, what people said and did, what worked and what did not, how people felt, and what might be done next. Trainers can explain children's needs at each age level and how programs meets those needs—for example, the rationale for arranging children's toys on shelves rather jumbling together in toy boxes. Trainers can also show how children of different ages use particular toys in different ways, and that sand, water, and other "messy" kinds of play are therapeutic for young children. Behavior guidance techniques can be demonstrated by role-playing.

Setting appropriate limits for children and guiding their behavior are matters of concern to all volunteers. Some may tend to permit unacceptable behavior "because the children have had such hard lives." In reality, however, condoning unacceptable behavior lowers children's self-esteem, and they begin to see themselves as unlovable and out-of-control. The basic premise of behavior guidance therefore is that it helps children develop high self-esteem when accomplished in positive, nonpunitive ways. Both volunteers and staff members can learn basic techniques of behavior guidance. (See Appendixes D and E.)

The third phase of training is supervised on-the-job training. During this session, volunteer trainees should observe children and teachers. At convenient times, supervisors can explain to volunteers reasons for doing specific things. Volunteers can question supervisors, and afterward they can discuss what has taken place. At succeeding sessions, volunteers can take on progressively more responsibilities. Volunteers' contacts with children should be limited to group activities for three to six months before allowing them to be alone with children. For liability reasons, many programs never allow volunteers to be alone with children. See the section below on risk management and program liability.

Volunteer Coordination and Support

Although volunteers can be used in a variety of capacities, they are effective only when a strong infrastructure of professional staff and organizational resources exists to support their work. In its study, *Volunteers 2000,* the American Red Cross [1989] found that the effective use of volunteer services required financial support. Agencies that use volunteers have to provide such services as task placement and supervision; such resources as pleasant workspaces, telephones, and typewriters; and such development incentives as training and career planning. These support services and resources are well worth the investment: NCJW estimates that every dollar invested in assisting volunteers generates four dollars in community services and resources [NCJW 1989].

Some people volunteer for projects or programs and are happy to take on whatever roles are available, but most volunteers come to programs with abilities and expertise that make them more suitable for some roles than for others. For example, some may be experts in public relations, or child rearing, or facilitating meetings—all of which may be valuable to particular programs. Programs should consider how to best match volunteers' abilities with program needs. Most programs assign tasks to volunteers on a trial basis; if matches do not work out, the programs give volunteers alternatives for volunteering in other locations.

Using volunteers' and staff members' range of abilities requires coordination in any program. Child care programs can successfully deal with the multifaceted needs of homeless children and their families only by carefully managing available resources. Problems with volunteer coordination waste resources, disrupt schedules, and increase tensions between volunteers and staff members—all of which negatively impact children in care. Coordinating volunteer resources requires a deliberate commitment of time from both staff members and volunteers themselves for training, feedback, and actual service.

Programs can be planned with flexibility in mind, but consistent scheduling is important. Volunteers must commit their time according to a calendar and understand that, when unexpected events come up for them, they have to arrange for substitutes. Most programs develop lists of substitute volunteers. Volunteers should inform supervisors of any changes in their schedules as soon as possible. Homeless children have traumatic lives to begin with and frequently become disappointed because adults have not been available for them when needed. It is important in the midst of the shelter experience that children know that adults are as predictable as possible.

Supervision

In smaller programs, directors can screen, orient, and train volunteers. Larger facilities usually have half- or full-time volunteer coordinators or resource people. Many program directors feel that separate volunteer coordinators are necessary to use volunteers effectively. In the survey, program directors who combined their volunteer coordinator positions with other responsibilities felt that their staff members were overworked and that having the positions stand alone would be more effective.

Volunteer coordinators exist in some programs as staff positions and in others as a volunteer positions. In most programs, staff members supervise volunteers who work with them. Board committees and other volunteers are supervised by board members or by shelter directors.

Because shelters are refuges for people in crisis, they are not stable environments. Client populations shift unpredictably, and volunteers must be able to assess situations quickly and adapt accordingly. Volunteers who overinvest in planned activities with particular children or groups in mind are apt to be disappointed. Working with families in crisis is stressful and emotionally draining. Because many of these families have complex, intergenerational problems, those who work with them experience a mixture of helplessness, confusion, anger, grief, satisfaction, and love. Care for caregivers is essential to help volunteers and staff members maintain good mental health and an ability to cope with stress. Volunteers need to review their experiences with supervisors regularly, either alone or in groups. Some programs have regular meetings that allow volunteers to reflect on their experiences and receive additional training. Training meetings can double as support groups for volunteers. Some programs use newsletters as sources of communication, affirmation, and information for volunteers. Newsletters can include schedules, monthly calendars, reminders about recent program decisions, and information on upcoming plans. They may also contain cartoons, short pertinent articles, and news related to individual volunteers, such as birthdays or accomplishments. Volunteers may even want to help produce these newsletters.

Volunteers need to be reminded frequently that they are important contributors to programs, either through meetings; newsletters; or more informal ways of communicating, such as on-the-spot recognition and opportunities to give feedback to supervisors. Additional ways of recognizing volunteers include articles in the media and appreciation dinners. Social activities like picnics and parties allow staff members and volunteers to get to know each other better and to develop a sense of teamwork.

Risk Management and Program Liability

Many programs institute risk management procedures to limit their exposure to liability claims. A commitment to running a high-quality program is probably the best insurance against litigation. Excellent adult-child ratios, an emphasis on retaining trained dependable staff members and volunteers, and listening to parents' concerns are hallmarks of high-quality child care.

Checking potential volunteers' records and never leaving volunteers alone with children are the most common risk management procedures. This means having staff members present even on field trips. Programs also carry liability insurance, obtain parent permission slips for field trips and photo releases, have liability waivers, and have disclaimers for incidents that happen outside sanctioned contexts—for example, transportation accidents.

Screening volunteer applicants to determine their suitability for programs is an essential part of the interview process. Apparent emotional instability should be noted. Extreme nervousness, fidgeting, distancing, or tuning out interviewers, or becoming angry and defensive at difficult subjects all can indicate that a person is not suited to the task of interacting with children. Interviewers' gut reactions to applicants should be considered during screening. Most often, if something "doesn't seem right" about the applicant, it isn't.

For example, pedophiles—adults who are sexually attracted to children—have an affinity for children who are emotionally needy. They may have held positions of trust such as scout masters, teachers, or camp counselors. Knowing that they are subject to police checks may deter some from pursuing volunteer positions in programs. Be aware, however, that most pedophiles do not have police records. They often have ingratiating manner that disarm protective adults in children's lives and create opportunities for abuse to occur.

Evaluation

Formally evaluating volunteers' experiences in a program, and staff members' experiences in working with volunteers, are crucial to determining how well volunteers are working in the program. When either a volunteer or the program terminates the volunteer's service, the volunteer coordinator or program director should conduct an exit interview. The volunteer experience can be looked upon as mutually beneficial, giving both volunteers and the staff members opportunities to grow and change. This gives both parties a sense of closure and completion. Volunteer coordinators or directors can determine whether volunteers' needs were met and gain information about their programs from volunteers' perspectives. Coordinators can determine if volunteers feel that they were adequately trained and learn what should be included in future training sessions.

In addition to exit interviews, shelter child care programs in the survey used other forms of volunteer evaluations. For example:

- They provide regular opportunities for volunteer feedback at meetings on program activities, concerns, and problem solving. Volunteer coordinators can write reports based on this feedback.

- They keep notebooks for comments from parents, volunteers, and other community partners.

- They conduct evaluations in staff meetings, in which staff members assess pros and cons of current volunteers and adjust task responsibilities accordingly.

Some programs may also consider using more formal techniques for assessing the value of volunteer efforts as a whole or the value of individual volunteers' efforts.[4] The traditional approach is an "effort evaluation," which involves compiling statistics on the number of volunteers involved in the program, the hours of volunteer service provided in a given period of time, and the number of clients served. This information sometimes is accompanied by a description of the extent to which volunteers' activities met program goals and affected clients' lives. This approach, however, does not include any explicit evaluation of the effectiveness of each volunteer's efforts.

To estimate replacement costs for equivalent services, programs may place monetary value on volunteers' activities, as if their services had been purchased from paid employees rather than provided by volunteers. To determine replacement costs, program managers identify paid employment classifications that are roughly equivalent to the types of services provided by volunteers in their programs. Hourly rates of pay for those employment classifications are multiplied by the number of volunteer hours to arrive at the monetary value of the volunteers' work. The cost of paid staff benefits and indirect service time also may be considered as part of this formula. This approach, however, implies the traditional idea that assessments of volunteer efforts can and should be translated into dollars without regard for intangible benefits that are valuable components of volunteer services.

A "naturalistic approach" to evaluation recognizes the unique relationships that volunteers can have with children and families in programs.[5] Volunteers can relate to children and families in different ways—more informally—than do professionals. This idea can be incorporated into the evaluation process by surveying children and families in programs with regard to how volunteers have affected them. Programs can thus evaluate the impacts of volunteers' activities on children's lives and describe the effects of volunteers' services on programs goals, using both qualitative and quantitative measures. This approach has the potential to evaluate the effectiveness of volunteers' efforts while avoiding measuring the value of volunteers' work in mere monetary terms.

Using Volunteers Successfully

Paying attention to details is crucial in using and managing volunteer programs. Training, supervision, support, communication, and evaluation can improve retention of volunteers and make recruiting new volunteers easier.

[4]   These ideas and terms are based on Curtis and Fisher [1989].
[5]   The term "naturalistic" is Curtis and Fisher's.

No matter how effectively programs use volunteers, however, volunteer efforts can never completely take the place of paid professionals. Rather than supplanting staff, volunteers extend their work and build programs' capacities. To be most effective, volunteers must have adequate supports by the programs in which they work.

Working in partnership with volunteer organizations is a particularly effective way to increase shelters' abilities to serve homeless children and their families and to generate community responses to the problems of homelessness. Volunteer organizations are good partners for several reasons:

- Relatively free of business and governmental constraints, volunteer organizations can risk supporting new and creative programs through community service.

- Volunteers identify and draw public attention to social problems and unmet community needs through public education.

- Volunteers' lack of self-interest often makes them more credible at advocacy than paid professionals, who often are seen as having vested interests.

Volunteers' activities frequently combine public education, community service, and advocacy. Volunteer organizations, for example, can act as political catalysts and community organizers. Their affiliations with ethnic and religious groups, business groups, social clubs, and government agencies, as well as their relatively neutral identities, enable them to be particularly effective at drawing community interests together around particular issues.

For shelter child care programs, developing working relationships with volunteer organizations can provide a steady flow of volunteers to work directly with children, a range of outside professional expertise to improve shelters' operations and management, and experienced groups of community leaders to serve on boards and to direct public attention toward necessary long-term solutions to homelessness. Good management practices and support resources for volunteers serving in these capacities can enable shelters to provide high-quality child care programs with abundant nurturing and education to help remedy the many difficulties that complicate the lives of homeless children.

References

Abdennur, A. (1987). *The conflict resolution syndrome: Volunteering, violence, and beyond.* Ottawa, ON: University of Ottawa Press

American Red Cross (1988). *Volunteers 2000.* Washington, DC: American Red Cross Publications.

Bellah, R.N. (1996). *Habits of the heart: Individualism and commitment in American life.* Berkeley: University of California Press.

Children's Defense Fund (CDF). (1991). *Homeless families: Failed policies and young victims.* Washington, DC: Author.

Curtis, K.M., & Fisher, J.E. (1989, Fall). Valuing volunteers: A naturalistic approach. *Journal of Volunteer Administration,* 11–20.

MacBride, M. (1982). *Step-by-step.* Bergen County, NJ: Volunteer Bureau of Bergen County.

Mergenhagen, P. (1991, June). A new breed of volunteer. *American Demographics, 13,* 54–55.

National Council of Jewish Women (NCJW). (1989). *Facts about volunteers: NCJW Center for the Child fact sheet.* New York: Author.

Office of Policy Research and Evaluation (OPRE), Program Analysis and Evaluation Division, and Enterprises for New Direction Inc. (1990). *Building better communities with student volunteers: An evaluation report on the student community service program.* Washington, DC: Office of Policy Research and Evaluation.

Points of Light Foundation. (1992). *Challenging the paradigm.* Washington, DC: Author.

Van Til, J. (1988). *Mapping the third sector: Voluntarism in a changing social economy.* New York: Foundation Center.

CHAPTER 9

Funding

Rachel Fesmire

Obtaining adequate funding to begin child care programs for children in shelters or to sustain ongoing programs is not an easy task. Currently, few funds are earmarked for children in shelters. Funding for children's services must compete with adult needs and housing projects. Shelter directors or designated staff members must become familiar with the various methods for acquiring funds. This chapter provides guidelines for funding activities, including developing program concepts, enlisting the active support of boards of directors, looking for funding in the private and public sectors, and writing proposals for funding.

Getting Started

The idea of starting a program for children will probably originate with shelter staff members, since they see the effects of children roaming shelters without focus and being taken from one office to the next by parents who have no child care arrangements. The first step, then, logically falls to shelter staff members or a committee with staff representation. Enlisting the aid of child development professionals from local colleges or universities to document the educational, health, and safety needs of children in shelters may be helpful. The committee should develop a clear vision for the program by answering four questions:

- What kind of program is needed?
- Should the program be located at the shelter or off site?
- Should the program serve children from more than one shelter?
- Should the program be exclusively for shelter children, or should it include other groups in the community?

Needs Assessment

To answer the first question, the committee should conduct a needs assessment. Who needs the services? Do most parents in the shelter need child care, or do only a few? Do they need care all day or just half the day? Can needs be met by contracting for space with community child care centers and family day care homes, or is it more appropriate to create a program that will meet the unique needs of these children and complement a parent support group in the shelter? Are specialized or therapeutic services needed for the children, such as on-site health care, play therapy, and transportation?

Location

If the committee decides to create a new program, plans must encompass selecting a location, staffing the program, obtaining equipment and materials, and acquiring licensing. Will the new program use volunteers, paraprofessionals, trained staff members, or some combination? When considering costs, plan two or three years ahead. How will the program be sustained beyond the first year of operation? If the space is on site, are renovations necessary? If the program is off site, is a search committee needed to find a building? Should the building be purchased or leased? How will the children be transported to an off-site facility? What local and state regulations apply to zoning, building, and fire codes and child care licensing?

Surveying local social service programs to see why some have succeeded and others have failed may be helpful. Ideally, this survey should include financial resources and in-kind contributions from volunteers, church groups, clubs, and other community organizations.

Community

The final two questions require a broader look at the community. Are there other groups with similar needs? For example, children who live in shelters are at high risk for abuse, and other children in the community may also be abused or at high risk. These children have the same needs for stability, safety, and appropriate play as the children in the shelter. Homeless children, children of low-income families, and victims of domestic violence or child abuse have common needs, especially in language development and in coping with their fear, grief, and anxiety. Combining efforts with other shelters, with state or local social service departments, or with local child abuse prevention groups may therefore be practical.

Creating child care programs is easier with flexible thinking. Be open to new ideas and different approaches. Be creative: Just because no one else has done it does not mean it will not work. Be willing to share turf and work with other agencies. Finally, whatever plan is decided upon will have to be one to which the shelter director and staff members can make a commitment to pursue.

Involving the Board of Directors

When a plan has been developed, put it on paper—it can be just a few pages in simple, direct language. State the goal: For instance, "To provide safe, developmentally appropriate care for children between the ages of 1 and 5 to enable parents to seek housing or jobs or to attend classes."

To build a case for the program, gather background information on child abuse and homelessness that fits the shelter's focus. Include statistics on the number and ages of the children served in the shelter. Explain why the program is important and what it will do for the parents and children. Show how establishing a new program relates to the overall mission of the shelter or agency.

Present this to the shelter's board of directors in a way that involves them in the project enthusiastically. Be prepared with specific ways the board can help. A rule of thumb is to conclude a presentation about needed money or resources with a list of what you need from them. This is the ideal time to say, "We are going to need a building" or "We are going to need a room, and we will need furnishings and equipment."

The makeup and role of boards may vary from one community and agency to the next. The shelter's day-to-day operations should be delegated to an agency director. Board members should spend their time and energy setting directions and developing policies for shelter programs and ensuring that fundraising goals are met.

Boards with responsibility for raising money should comprise movers and shakers in the community. Identify and put on the board people with histories of making contributions to similar community projects. They might include bankers, accountants, attorneys, business chief executives, advertising agents, key representatives of marketing firms or insurance companies, members of the media, and people from civic groups such as the Junior League or the Medical Auxiliary.

Boards comprising carefully selected members will do most of the fundraising. Ask them to identify potential private and public funding sources and to go with you or to make contacts for you. Let board members set up appointments. Remember, people give to people. Most people respond favorably to personal contact. Be prepared to meet with people that you or your board identify as having needed skills or resources.

Sources of Funding

Private and public funds are available to support programs for homeless and at-risk children and families. Private funding can come from businesses; churches; service clubs, such as Rotary, Kiwanis, Altrusa, the Junior League, and Civitans; the local United Way; private foundations; and individuals. Public funds are available at the county, state, and federal levels. Tax-exempt status (501[c]) and licensing for children's programs are required for eligibility for most of these funds.

Private Funding Sources

The first place to look for funding is your own backyard. Most communities have community and family foundations. Even though they usually give small amounts of money, a grant of $500 or $1,000 can be essential in getting a program off the ground. Often, local foundations support programs over time; regional, state, or national foundations are unlikely to stick with programs for more than two or three years. Additionally, getting small community foundations to give to your program adds validity when approaching larger foundations.

People in the community who share your goals and have relationships with your organization may be willing to make personal contributions to the project. They will have friends and contacts whom they can recruit as well.

Contact businesses in the community to find out if they support community projects. For example, one major retail chain gives money to its stores every year to be used for community projects chosen by the employees. Another major corporation encourages its employees to participate actively in community projects. Many companies match employee donations to nonprofits. These contributions may be small, but they add up.

The United Way provides funding for many shelters and child care scholarships. Most United Way agencies have someone on staff who is designated to look at community planning needs and make recommendations for funding and venture grants. Contact your local United Way to find out about eligibility for funding and guidelines for proposals.

In addition to civic groups such as the Junior League and Kiwanis, approach garden clubs, book clubs, homemakers' clubs, and religious groups. Write to these groups and describe your program and the community needs it will meet. Ask to meet with the clubs and determine where the project fits into their priorities.

Some clubs traditionally give scholarships. Calculate the cost of a scholarship for one slot for a month, a quarter, and a year. This allows a club to select an amount that is more manageable so they can become involved in providing child care services or play therapy to a child who is homeless or has been the victim of domestic violence. A large portion of funding may come from scholarships if a number of clubs agree to participate in this way.

Preparing a Proposal

Make the proposal short and to the point. Give enough detail so the funder has a clear picture of what the organization wants to do and how this will be implemented. Include the following information:

- A brief description of the project. What will it do and who will it serve?

- The need for the project. How does it relates to the organization's other work, and what unmet needs will it fill?

- The project's goals. Be clear about what you expect to achieve.

- Strategies the organization will use to reach these goals.

- A project timeline. What will the organization do, month by month, to accomplish its goals?

- Expected outcomes or impacts. Who, and how many, will benefit from the project?

- Information about the organization and the people who will carry out the project. This will help establish credibility.

- Information about local or community support that the organization has already obtained. Include other contributions, volunteers, and letters of support.

- A plan for evaluating the project.

- A detailed budget.

- Answers to specific concerns and priorities of the funder.

The Foundation Center publishes *The Foundation Center's Guide to Proposal Writing,* a valuable resource for anyone writing proposals. It can be ordered from The Foundation Center, 79 Fifth Avenue, Eighth Floor, New York, NY 10003-3016; 212/620-4230, FAX 212/807-3677.

Consider also the value of nonmonetary community resources, particularly the value of volunteers. As Chapter 8 points out, a core group of volunteers who can be trained and depended upon can contribute greatly to the success of a program. Foundations often want to know what kind of community support a program is getting. By keeping track of volunteer hours and activities, as well as donations of goods and services, you can calculate a monetary value and demonstrate community support in a concrete way.

State and National Foundations

Public and college libraries usually have directories that list national and state foundations with examples of projects they have funded. The Internet site for the Council on Foundations (www.cof.org) is extremely helpful in identifying possible sources of funding and in developing proposals.

Once you have identified foundations that support projects similar to yours, send for guidelines and proposal due dates. Review lists of previously awarded grants to determine the most likely level of funding. Don't ask a foundation that gives grants of $50,000 a year for a grant of $250,000!

Write a letter of inquiry to appropriate foundations to test their interest in your project. If possible, arrange meetings with their project officers. Foundations know one another's priorities and can often suggest other places to try if they themselves are not interested. If a foundation is interested, the project officer can guide you through the proposal stage.

State and Federal Funds

There is little predictable, stable funding at the federal or state levels for homeless children and families and the programs that serve them.

In 1996, Congress passed the Personal Responsibility and Work Opportunity Reconciliation Act (P.L. 104-193), popularly known as welfare reform, which made massive changes in federal law regarding welfare and other human service programs. Most of the entitlement programs that assisted homeless children and families—such as Aid to Families with Dependent Children (AFDC), the Job Opportunities and Basic Skills Training Program, and emergency assistance—were eliminated by the new law and replaced by state-funded programs using Temporary Assistance for Needy Families (TANF) block grants. States may use a portion of their TANF funds to pay for child care; however, this child care is primarily for children of "needy" parents who work 20 hours or more weekly. Families who use homeless shelters are unlikely to fall into this category.

Families are eligible for assistance using federal TANF funds for a maximum of five years in their lifetimes. Using their own funds, states may, at their option, choose to continue assistance beyond this limit. The prospects for this, however, vary from state to state. Illegal immigrants continue to be ineligible for public welfare, and benefits for legal immigrants have been cut by more than $22 billion. States can provide or deny TANF, Medicaid, and Title XX benefits to legal immigrants residing in the United States on the enactment date, August 22, 1996. Noncitizens who arrive in the country after that date are denied most federal means-tested benefits for five years.

Child care is no longer an entitlement for current and former AFDC recipients. Title XX—the Social Services Block Grant—which has been used to subsidize children in center-based and family child care, was cut 15% for FY 1997 and is likely to be cut again for FY 1998. The Child Care and Development Block Grant (CCDBG), passed in 1996, consolidated the funds from the child care entitlement programs and the old CCDBG. States may transfer up to 30% of their TANF funds to CCDBG. If Congress appropriates the full amount for CCDBG each year, there will be an estimated $6 billion more between 1996 and 2002 for child care than the states spent in 1995.

The most likely source of CCDBG funding for homeless children and families and the programs that serve them is the General Entitlement and Remainder funds section of CCDBG. Legislation stipulates that no less than 70% of this money must be used for child care assistance to families who received assistance under Title IV-A of the Social Security Act, which was eliminated in October 1996 under welfare reform. The priority for CCDBG money is to assist families who are attempting, through work activities, to transition off assistance, and to help families who are at risk of becoming dependent. A substantial portion of the remaining amounts will be used to provide assistance to other low-income working families. Obviously, this "substantial portion" will vary from state to state. In states where most families are working to transition off assistance, those families who are unable to do so will be placed at the bottom of the funding ladder.

Another possible funding source is the Supplemental Assistance for Facilities to Assist the Homeless section of the Stewart B. McKinney Homeless Assistance Act. This program is administered by the Office of Community Planning and Development at the U.S. Department of Housing and Urban Development. It includes a provision for assistance to meet the special needs of homeless families with children. Again, the focus of this legislation is not solely on children, but on facilities. There will probably be strong competition for funds for homeless families and children.

For funding and services for individual children, contact state and local Head Start agencies and departments of mental health, education, and health. Head Start serves the poorest children in communities and has begun to operate programs specifically targeted to serve homeless children and families. Mental health departments serve special-needs children age 3 and under, whereas departments of education serve special-needs children age 4 through 21. Health departments can provide immunizations and health screenings and may help run medical clinics in shelters. Although funds from these agencies must remain with the programs for which the funds are provided—for example, Head Start money must stay with Head Start—individual programs will not have to raise the funds for the services they provide.

People responsible for fundraising for children's programs must be knowledgeable about state and local plans for available funds and keep close contact with those who disburse these funds. This relationship, nurtured over time, is key to being considered when new funds are authorized or innovative programs are begun.

Federal grants are also a possible source of funding. Check the *Federal Register* or the *Commerce Business* daily for announcements. You can ask to be put on the *Federal Register's* mailing list for particular Requests for Proposals (RFPs). To answer an RFP, follow the directions for submission as closely as possible. Time is usually short for responding to proposals, so move quickly. Include letters of support from key local groups.

An Ongoing Process

Developing funding resources is an ongoing process. A funding plan can be helpful; following this plan is critical, as are periodic reviews and assessments. To do a thorough job, stay knowledgeable about all potential funding sources. Remember the goals and purpose of the program, and weigh the potential funding source requirements against the program's mission. Don't just chase available money! Make sure these requirements contribute to meeting your goals and don't require such extensive modification so as to compromise the integrity of the program.

Additional Sources of Information

The best source of information on foundations in the United States is the Foundation Center in New York City. The center is located on the Internet at http://fdncenter.org. Some of the center's materials include

- *The Foundation Directory.* Contains brief information on over 7,500 foundations that hold assets of at least $2 million or distribute $200,000 or more in grants annually.

- *The Foundation Directory, Part 2.* Covers more than 5,000 foundations with assets between $1 million and $2 million, or annual grant programs between $50,000 and $200,000.

- *The Foundation Grants Index.* Lists grants of $10,000 or more for a given year for the country's 1,000 largest foundations.

- *User-Friendly Guide to Funding Research and Resources: INTERNET EDITION.* Popular resource available on the Internet at http://fdncenter.org/onlib/ufgtoc.html.

For more information, contact the Foundation Center, 79 Fifth Avenue, Eighth Floor, New York, NY 10003-3016; 212/620-4230, FAX 212/807-3677.

C H A P T E R

Programs for Children in Shelters: An Overview

Following is an overview of selected programs established to meet the needs of children and families in shelters. Program descriptions include discussions of how the programs got started, as well as each program's goals, administrative structures and staffing, and demographics.

The Vogel Alcove, Dallas, Texas

Beverly A. Mulvihill and Andra McBain

In the mid-1980s, the Social Action Committee of Congregation Shearith Israel, a conservative synagogue in Dallas, Texas, was helping homeless people by serving meals to residents of one shelter. To expand this mission and address the problems of homelessness on a broader scale, in May 1986, the committee called upon the entire Jewish community to begin devising a plan to deal with the problems of homeless families in Dallas. In response, 21 organizations agreed to be the founding members of a coalition that came to be known as the Dallas Jewish Coalition for the Homeless (DJCH). Since its inception, DJCH has grown to 29 member organizations. The coalition provides a vehicle through which the Jewish community can work to alleviate the plight of homeless people in Dallas.

Based on further discussions with community leaders and professionals, the committee formed task forces on child care, housing, jobs, health services, and hunger. In studying their respective areas and making recommendations to the full committee, the task forces documented the fact that child care was the only one of the five areas in which no services were available to Dallas's homeless population. Because such services were lacking, children were being left in cars, taken with parents on endless rounds of appointments and interviews, and often left on their own. Thus, in November 1986, DJCH chose child care as its total focus. Through supportive, nurturing, quality day care for infants and children living in area shelters, DJCH hoped to provide children with stability and security and allow parents to concentrate on obtaining job training and employment that would lead to eventual economic independence.

Administrative Structure and Funding

DJCH set a goal of raising $250,000 to fund a two-year pilot project of quality child care. With most of its fundraising goal met, the coalition opened the first Alcove In March 1987. Initially, the Alcove served 12 children, from infancy through age 5, in one downtown shelter for homeless families. The facility quickly expanded to serve 21 infants and preschool children, while approximately 30 school-age children participated in an after-school program in cooperation with the Young Women's Christian Association (YWCA) of Metropolitan Dallas. During the summer, the YWCA provided a full-day, school-age program. Within a year, the coalition was serving eight shelters and transitional housing programs. In the first two years, DJCH used these two facilities to house programs for more than 1,000 children of homeless families in Dallas.

DJCH contracted with the YWCA until the fall of 1994 to provide professional staff for the Vogel Alcove. In 1994, DJCH assumed full management responsibilities for the program and now owns and operates Vogel Alcove. The professional staff is supplemented by an active and valuable volunteer program. Monthly report meetings help maintain coordination among the coalition, the child care staff, and the client agencies served by the program. These meetings assist in the collection of statistics and confront problems that may arise. In addition, a professional advisory committee, consisting of experts in early childhood education, child development, social work, psychology, and related fields, makes recommendations to enhance the curriculum and classroom environment.

DJCH administrative staff members spend approximately 45% of their time in fundraising activities, such as grant writing or coordinating the Vogel Alcove Annual Arts Event, which provides up to 40% of annual operating funds. Many individuals have contributed time, expertise, and funds to the project; and the support of local and national foundations and corporations have allowed the project to grow and meet increasing needs.

The Present Program

In 1989, DJCH consolidated all of the child care programs in a new location. The program was renamed the Vogel Alcove in honor of Thelma and Philip Vogel, who were instrumental in forming the DJCH and who died in a plane crash in 1988. A 4,500 square-foot warehouse was remodeled into a child care facility that could serve infants through school-age children. Grants from such Dallas institutions as the Hoblitzelle Foundation, the NCH Corporation, and the Zale Foundation, as well as contributions of materials and labor from businesses and individuals in the community, made the new center possible.

The Vogel Alcove was able to serve up to 85 children in this location, from age 6 weeks through 12 years, until 1995, when DJCH purchased and renovated an 11,000-square-foot facility into a state-of-the-art child development and social services center. The Vogel Alcove now provides free child care for 102 homeless children ages 6 weeks to 6 years. Lead supporters of the new Vogel Alcove center included the Meadows Foundation of Texas and the Hillcrest Foundation. In 1992, DJCH helped the local school district open a year-round after-school program in the Alcove's neighborhood.

The Vogel Alcove is open Monday through Friday, 7:00 A.M. to 6:00 P.M. Licensed by the state of Texas, the Vogel Alcove received accreditation by the National Association for the Education of Young Children in 1997. The average length of enrollment is 20 weeks. The work of the Vogel Alcove has touched the lives of over 5,600 children since its inception.

Children and their families are referred from 16 Dallas-area homeless assistance programs. These affiliate agencies must contract with DJCH and have as their primary goal economic independence for the families they serve.

The program's overall purpose is to provide quality child care for homeless families so they may achieve economic independence and emotional recovery. By making accessible, quality child care available, DJCH enables parents to work, seek employment or job training, and acquire affordable housing. In addition, the Vogel Alcove provides a secure and stable environment so that children can overcome the trauma of homelessness. Toward this goal, the program

- offers each child, ages 2 to 6 years, play therapy with a licensed social worker, which helps children identify and express their feelings about issues of abuse and neglect, and the anxiety that comes with the uncertainty of being a homeless child;

- provides developmentally appropriate curricula, environments, and activities;

- identifies and provides on-site assistance for children with developmental delays in speech and language and cognitive, physical, emotional, and social development; and

- provides case management, crisis intervention, parent education, and family support groups for all families with children enrolled in the program and for one year after leaving the Vogel Alcove.[1]

---

[1] Provided by the Crystal Charity Ball organization.

Figure 1. Volgel Alcove			
Group	**Age**	**Maximum number of children**	**Staff-child ratio**
Infants	6 weeks to 14 months	8	1:4
Toddler I	14 to 24 months	10	1:5
Toddler II	2 to 3 years	12	1:6
Preschool	3 to 6 years	16	1:8
Get Well	any age	8	1:4

Homeless Outreach Medical Services of Parkland Hospital provides a twice-weekly on-site pediatric clinic. Health services are also available daily through the Vogel Alcove's Get Well program, which provides a pediatric nurse each morning for health checks, and daily care plans for children who, by state child care standards, would not be able to attend their regular classrooms. The Get Well room has its own specially trained staff members and a separate ventilation system to prevent the spread of infection. Parents can then continue their jobs or training programs without interruption when their children are recovering from the many illnesses that young homeless children experience.

The Vogel Alcove program is sensitive to the specific needs of homeless children and therefore maintains a child-staff ratio far surpassing minimum licensing standards. As Figure 1 shows, the Vogel Alcove child care program is divided into five groups and has a total of 10 classrooms.

The Vogel Alcove makes every effort to secure the best-qualified staff available. At minimum, lead teachers must have either an associate's degree in child development or a related field, or a child development associate degree (CDA) with at least five years' experience. Assistant caregivers must be working toward a CDA and have a minimum of two years' experience. The Vogel Alcove staff receives special training to work with homeless children and their parents. Social service staff, mental health, early childhood, and health care professionals consult with the staff on a voluntary basis.

Paid staff members' work with children is augmented by a group of trained volunteers from DJCH member organizations, the Dallas County Community Colleges, public and private schools, Foster Grandparents, corporations, and the community at large.

DJCH has provided a significant service to countless children and families. The commitment and dedication of volunteers, board members, and paid staff working in partnership with other community groups has made it possible for the Vogel Alcove to alleviate the plight of homeless families in Dallas.

The Ark, Baltimore, Maryland

Pat Gallagher

In 1989, Action for the Homeless, a Baltimore advocacy organization, gathered together a group of public and private agencies serving homeless people to identify gaps in services to homeless families, to develop programs to fill those gaps, and to attract funding for the new programs. This group evolved into the Coalition for Homeless Children and Families. Shortly thereafter, the Abell Foundation in Baltimore became a member and one of several funding sources for the coalition. After reviewing reports from local emergency shelters, the coalition concluded that the most apparent need was a system of services for homeless children of all ages. The coalition made day care for homeless children a top priority.

Another local group, Episcopal Social Ministries (ESM), also realized the need for a day care program for children of homeless families. ESM has been actively involved in helping homeless people since 1986 when it opened Bethany, Baltimore's first transitional housing program for intact families, followed in 1987 by Phoenix Place, the first transitional housing program in Baltimore for abused and battered women and their children. But these transitional programs were small, and ESM was experiencing an increase in the number of young children who needed services. ESM realized that parents need to be out during the day to keep appointments with sources for housing, social services, job training, and job searches. These difficult tasks were made even more difficult for parents because they had to take their young children along. Youngsters were spending their days on transit buses, in waiting rooms, and with their parents at appointments. For this reason, ESM began to develop plans for the Ark, a model day care program for homeless preschool children. When the Coalition for Homeless Children and Families and ESM learned of each other's efforts, they joined forces, and ESM became a coalition member.

The Ark opened its doors in 1990; but to make the Ark a reality, the coalition first had to make many decisions about practical issues: what shelters to serve, how to provide transportation, and how to select families to participate. Through a generous donation, the YWCA, the coalition's lead agency, purchased a bus to transport children between the shelters and the Ark. Coalition members wanted to ensure that children would spend less than an hour on the bus. This affects the number of shelters served as well as the distance shelters can be from the Ark. Each shelter served by the Ark decides which families in that shelter should be served, based on parents' interests, children's ages, and appropriateness of the program for individual families and children. Shelter staff members are encouraged to enroll children whose parents most need respite, as well as children who appear to have developmental delays.

Funding

Start-up funding for the Ark came from a variety of sources, including the United Way, local community foundations, and ESM. A number of local community foundations and corporations helped the Ark obtain $88,000 for building renovations, $13,000 for start-up equipment, and funds to meet the initial annual operating budget of $125,000.

In fiscal year 1995–1996, the Ark received 39% of its operating budget from corporate and foundation sponsors, 19% from public funds, and 6% from parishes. The remainder of the budget was met through unrestricted contributions to ESM's annual giving campaign. Although the Ark had hoped to receive significant funding through a publicly funded purchase-of-care day care voucher system, only a handful of children have been eligible for vouchers during the time they were enrolled. The YWCA continues to receive funds to provide transportation. Other coalition partners provide in-kind services, such as on-site health screenings, play therapy, and developmental screenings.

The Program

The Ark operates in the undercroft of Baltimore's Episcopal Church of the Resurrection, built in 1924. The congregation received the Ark warmly, due in part to their relationship with ESM and their familiarity with the Ark's program manager, the rector at the church. The congregation and ESM already had a working relationship since the transitional housing program was, and continues to be, located in the rectory.

The undercroft underwent much renovation to prepare space for the Ark. Volunteers from the Neighborhood Design Center—a nonprofit agency of architects, engineers, interior designers, contractors, and others who volunteer their services at little or no cost—assisted in planning the renovations. The main area is a very large room. Creative use of furnishings breaks the space into smaller activity areas for children and space for adults. The adult space is used variously as a staff lounge, a parent space, and a doctor's office on Tuesday mornings for physicals for new children. It is also the gathering place and lecture hall for groups who want to see the program in action. The children's space makes use of soft, muted colors to prevent overstimulation. It was designed for versatility, because the church uses it every weekend for fellowship and several times a year for festivals or dinners.

The Ark serves preschool children between the ages of 2 and 5 living in Baltimore shelters. It provides a quality early childhood education program for 20 children. Since its first year, the Ark has served an average of 70 or more children per year. Various shelters, including night and emergency shelters, transitional shelters, and shelters for battered women use the program.

Shelter staff members play active roles in helping children enroll in the Ark. They provide the first information parents receive about the program. They initiate the intake process for enrollment, then confirm with the Ark's parent involvement specialist. The bus begins making its rounds at 8:00 A.M., and the children arrive at 9:00 A.M. At 3:00 P.M., the children are transported back to their shelters.

The Ark is a fully licensed program and therefore must have health inventories and immunization records on file for all children. Appointments at most clinics for well-baby check-ups are frequently scheduled six weeks from the dates of request. The pediatric nurse from the Children's Health Outreach Program (CHOP) at Baltimore's Mercy Medical Center has been instrumental in obtaining earlier appointments for some children. A pediatrician from nearby Johns Hopkins University Hospital conducts physicals at the Ark for new children every Tuesday morning.

The Maryland Department of Human Resources (DHR), the state licensing agency for child care, has helped with difficulties in obtaining immunization records. At times, parents have had difficulty locating their children's immunization records, which frequently get lost as families move. DHR allows the Ark to place in children's files a copy of a letter requesting immunizations from their health care providers. This allows children to start before the Ark receives the records.

Staffing and Support Services

The Ark has four full-time staff members: the director, a senior staff person, a parent involvement specialist, and an aide. Volunteers help a few days each week. All of the Ark's staff members exceed DHR's requirements for number of years of experience, and some have additional education. In choosing staff members, the Ark considers applicants who express a desire not only to work with young children, but also to work with homeless people. Salaries are on the moderate side for the child care staff, but the benefit package includes generous paid vacation and sick leave, excellent health benefits, and life insurance. Continuing training is encouraged, with a minimum number of training hours required; the Ark pays staff members' expenses for training.

Although ESM is the sponsoring agency for the Ark, the entire coalition is instrumental in providing support services. The YWCA uses the services of a transportation company to transport the children between the shelters and the Ark. CHOP provides pediatric health care services both at the Ark and at the shelters. Health Care for the Homeless was instrumental in recruiting the volunteer services of pediatricians from Johns Hopkins.

Although the primary tie with other service organizations is through the coalition, other groups have expressed interest in working with the Ark in a variety of ways. The University of Maryland provides young volunteers through its community service program. A teacher associated with a drug abuse program sponsored by Johns Hopkins works with the children weekly. A local sorority plans special activities four times a year for the children. A clown visits monthly and tells stories, does face painting, and has other fun activities. A storyteller-puppeteer-accordion player delights the children once a month. A group referred to as "The Dinosaur Ladies" comes monthly for a variety of activities about dinosaurs.

The Ark's Philosophy

The Ark provides a secure, stable, predictable environment where children have plenty of time to play and be children. Through play, children sort through their difficulties and experiment with interacting in safe settings. Learning, too, occurs through play. As children come to the Ark, they are eager to explore their new environment. The Ark gives them plenty of time to explore this world and enjoy themselves.

Children are enrolled in the Ark program for an average of eight weeks. The goals, therefore, must be basic but essential to the children's future learning. The Ark's goals seek to:

- **Promote positive self-esteem for each child.** The Ark accomplishes this by providing many opportunities for positive interaction with adults who respect each child's uniqueness. Staff members create scrapbooks for each child, containing photographs of the child at the center, as well as the child's art work. The scrapbooks become a good-bye gift to the family.

- **Assist each child in developing self-control through nonpunitive guidance.** The program offers choices to children within limits: for example, "Do you want to paint at the easel or make a puzzle?" Caregivers use "if-then" statements to explain the consequences of actions. The program has a structured daily schedule, but staff members talk about changes in the schedule, such as trips to the library or birthday parties, prior to each event special.

- **Encourage a sense of trust in each child** by providing a structured and predictable environment, including space, time, and routines. Children are involved in decision making.

- **Create situations that allow each child to experience positive social interactions with adults and other children.** Staff members try to have enough materials available to minimize waiting for turns. They also provide lots of appropriate positive physical contact.

- **Provide a variety of developmentally appropriate activities and experiences for each child.** The program sets short-term goals for the children, based on individual abilities and needs. An indoor activity gym provides for gross-motor activities, with small wheel toys readily available. The program also provides many opportunities for language development.

Parent Activities

The Ark holds occasional parent sessions and tries to provide parents with opportunities to enjoy being with their children and to have activities they might not otherwise have while living in a shelter. At Halloween, for example, parents are invited to accompany the children to pick out pumpkins and carve them. Parents are invited to dye Easter eggs, decorate cookies, paint at the easel, and build with blocks. The generosity of supporters enables parents to Christmas-shop for their children each year. Parents can also choose birthday gifts for their children form the many toys that have been donated. Wrapping paper, ribbon, and tape are provided so parents can wrap their gifts for their children.

The program does not monitor parents' activities in any way. Although staff members encourage parents to participate in parent-child activities, attendance is not mandatory as a condition of their children's enrollment at the Ark. Although the Ark's primary focus is its children, the program benefits parents as well. The most obvious benefit to parents is in providing opportunities to conduct business without young children under foot.

The Ark provides a refuge for children where they can come during the day; a place where they can experience a bit of childhood happiness; a place where they can laugh, play, and be children. The Ark is able to continue its work on behalf of young children because many people support the program in so many ways.

Homeless Children's Network, Seattle, Washington

Jean Bombardier

The Homeless Children's Network (HCN) was established in 1989 with a grant from the U.S. Department of Health and Human Services to the Seattle Department of Housing and Human Services. The project's primary purpose has been to establish a system for linking homeless preschool children in family shelters and transitional housing with community child care programs. HCN provides child care placements and works with homeless families to help children access developmental assessments and other early childhood education services, including services for children with special needs.

To implement this project, HCN organized a planning committee comprising representatives from key agencies serving high-risk families, including shelters, Health Care for the Homeless, and child care providers. Continuous communication and monthly coordination with child care providers and shelters for homeless families has been crucial to the success of HCN services. City funds, combined with funding from Family Services (a countywide social service agency) and corporate and individual donors, support a coordinator to manage HCN and the child care linkage and referral program. The city funds transportation services. HCN is housed at Family Services.

In June 1996, the City of Seattle and King County submitted a consolidated application for a three-year grant from the U.S. Department of Housing and Urban Development (HUD) under the Stewart B. McKinney Homeless Assistance Act. Child care for homeless families, including child care vouchers and transportation services, was one of 11 projects funded. King County is the lead administrative agency.

Services

HCN offers services to homeless families and shelter providers. HCN originally served child care providers also, but this group is currently served by King County Child Care and the City of Seattle Comprehensive Child Care Program.

Homeless families

To achieve independence, homeless parents need safe appropriate care for their children while they seek or maintain employment, attend treatment, seek permanent housing, or obtain respite from the stress in their lives. Because parents are preoccupied with meeting survival needs, they often need considerable help getting their children enrolled in and transported to child care. HCN staff members help families find suitable child care for their children and help them find funding through the state welfare agency or by providing vouchers. Children who need specialized assessments are scheduled for appointments through the state Office of Developmental Disabilities or the Seattle Public School District's Child Find program. HCN arranges transportation for these appointments when necessary.

HCN staff members see continuity of care as vital for these children, who experience constant disruption in their living arrangements, with particular emphasis on securing long-term stable care through federal and state funds or city subsidies.

Shelter providers

HCN maintains a catalogue of resources and has access to information about openings in quality child care programs throughout the city. To share updated information about child care resources, and to identify families needing child care assistance, HCN has regular contact with all participating shelters. Once child care is found, HCN follows up with shelter providers to determine the effectiveness of the services provided.

Of the 14 emergency shelters and transitional housing programs that use HCN services, four are domestic violence shelters. In addition, five programs that provide vouchers for shelter use HCN's services. Eight agencies that provide other homeless services, and 10 to 20 agencies that provide miscellaneous services, also call HCN for resources. The shelters range in size from 15 to 90 beds. Half of the shelters employ children's advocates or offer some type of respite child care on site.

Child care providers

Services available to child care providers through King County's and the City of Seattle's child care programs include staff training, curriculum development, on-site child health assessments, child mental health care, staff consultations, and assistance with grant writing. Staff training covers such topics as child abuse, grief and loss, child development, early childhood education, nutrition, and anti-bias and culturally relevant curriculum. Learning materials designed to meet the special needs of homeless children are also available.

Programs

HCN originally had five dedicated child care slots for homeless children from birth to school age. Paying for the slots guaranteed child care providers at least the same rate of reimbursement as full-paying families who are not homeless, despite a possible high rate of absenteeism. Over the years, as the use of these slots decreased, monthly vouchers for use at 150 child care programs throughout the city grew in popularity because they provided more choice and convenience for the families. These child care homes and centers contracted with the City of Seattle to provide voucher child care service. The city sets high quality standards, and annual assessments help maintain these standards. HCN now maintains two dedicated slots at a family child care home that is licensed for 12 children. This provider has a child development associate credential and is experienced in both Head Start and family child care programs.

Two programs, Our Place Child Care Center and Morningsong, offer care to homeless children exclusively. Morningsong, also sponsored by Family Services, is located at a family shelter and serves predominantly children from that shelter. Our Place is a collaborative effort serving children from five shelters. These two programs serve a total of 38 children, ages 12 months to 6 years. They are open year-round from 8:30 A.M. to 5:30 P.M., Monday through Friday.

The distance between shelters and child care sites varies from 1 1/2 to 8 miles. HCN offers many different options for transportation, including single-use bus tickets, monthly bus passes, gas vouchers, and taxi and van service vouchers. This allows parents to transport their children to and from child care and to travel to and from such activities as seeking employment; attending job training, medical and mental health appointments, and parenting classes; and seeking permanent housing.

HCN's resource development component brings together volunteers from the community to administer a variety of education and awareness activities. The Baby Boutique, an attractive clothing bank for infants and young children of homeless families, is staffed entirely by volunteers. Common Cents is an annual awareness and donation drive that solicits monetary contributions for homeless families from elementary school children. The project is staffed by a Jesuit volunteer; over 50 elementary schools participate each year.

Disposable diapers for homeless families with infants and small children are always in great demand. HCN now has a volunteer diaper committee coordinator who oversees numerous successful diaper drives annually and helps find corporate sponsors and other sources of funding to help fill this huge need.

HCN and other organizations that serve the homeless population host The Share Your Care Fair, an annual awareness and entertainment event. Both homeless families and those who have homes are treated to an array of activities, including entertainment, food, children's health and development screenings, and a newly developed interactive exhibit that demonstrates the plight of homelessness.

Recommendations

HCN has learned that successful child care services for homeless children should include a number of factors:

- Providers in regular licensed child care programs need specialized training prior to serving homeless children.
- Make ongoing training and mental health consultations available as needed.
- Try to locate programs in close proximity to shelters for greater convenience and more affordable transportation.
- Provide transportation in the form of bus passes, gas vouchers, or taxi or van vouchers if possible.
- Provide infant slots to accommodate the high demand for infant care.
- Provide a low child-to-caregiver ratio.
- Try to keep children in the same child care program, even when the family moves, to provide continuity and stability for the children.
- Offer parent education and support groups.

Head Start Demonstration Programs

Adele Richardson Ray and Thelma Harms

Head Start has a long history of serving homeless children and families using a variety of models. The following examples illustrate the variety of Head Start's targeted services:

- Head Start of the Catholic Charities of the Archdiocese of Chicago brings homeless children and parents from several city shelters to one shelter with a classroom and parent resource room.
- The Santa Clara, California, Family Living Center operates a Head Start program for homeless children, eight hours a day, four days a week, year-round.
- Bucks County Head Start in Pennsylvania operates a home-based program for homeless families in community shelters.
- The Martin Luther King Jr. Head Start program in Baltimore runs a Parent-Child Center for infants and toddlers on the first floor of a transitional housing facility.
- The Episcopal Community Services Head Start in Chula Vista, California, coordinates services for homeless families, working with the Salvation Army and other agencies to secure emergency family assistance, a local mental health

clinic to obtain substance abuse counseling for parents, the public schools to facilitate children's transition to elementary school, and area transitional housing programs.

- Head Start and HUD jointly funded the Seattle Expanded Child Care Project to increase the stability and self-sufficiency of homeless and disadvantaged families.

In fiscal year 1993, the Administration for Children, Youth, and Families (ACYF) earmarked up to $3 million to increase the capacity of Head Start grantees to serve the special needs of homeless families and children in their Head Start service areas [ACYF 1992]. Project awards ranged from $75,000 to $200,000 per year. At least 20% of the total cost of the demonstration project had to come from sources other than the federal government. Projects were funded for three years.

An essential component of Head Start demonstration projects is collaboration with community and state resources for homeless children and families, especially programs under the Stewart B. McKinney Homeless Assistance Act.

The goals of the demonstration program were to

- enable additional homeless families to access Head Start services,
- provide services that are responsive to the special needs of homeless children and families,
- identify effective methods of responding to the needs of homeless families, and
- implement and document replicable strategies for collaboration between Head Start programs and community agencies on behalf of homeless families.

Projects applying for the demonstration program were required to include strategies

- to identify and recruit homeless children and families;
- to maintain continuity of services for families and children if they moved to other communities;
- to meet the needs of children and families in the areas of health, housing, employment, parenting skills, and social support;
- to meet the mental health needs of children, families, and staff members; and
- to integrate the staff members of all Head Start components to meet the needs of homeless children and families.

An evaluation design was also required.

Homeless Project Grantees

In 1993–94, 17 projects received grants. The demonstration phase of this project ended in September 1996. In June 1996, under a congressional set-aside, the 17 programs received a one-year transition grant to be administered by the regional Head Start office; $3.2 million has been allocated for 1996–97—approximately $200,000 per program, although the size of the grant varies by program size. Programs must maintain the quality and content of the original programs but can change the program design. After the transitional year, the allocation will be folded into local Head Start programs' regular program budgets.

The homeless project grantees include

- Parents in Community Action, Inc.
  700 Humboldt Avenue North
  Minneapolis, MN 55411

- United Planning Organization
  810 Potomac Avenue SE
  Washington, DC 20003

- Bright Beginnings
  Georgetown University
  901 Rhode Island Avenue NW
  Washington, DC 20001

- Human Resources Administration
  30 Main Street
  Brooklyn, NY 11201

- Community Services Agency
  P.O. Box 10167
  Reno, NV 89510

- Southwest Human Development
  202 East Earl Drive, #140
  Phoenix, AZ 85012

- Westchester Community Opportunity Program, Inc.
  2269 Saw Mill River Road, Building 3
  Elmsford, NY 10523

- Action for Boston Community Development
  178 Tremont Street
  Boston, MA 02111

- City of Chicago Department of Human Services
  510 North Peshtigo Court
  Chicago, IL 60611

- City of Oakland Head Start Program
  505 14th Street, Suite 300
  Oakland, CA 94612

- Hawkeye Area Community Action Program
  P.O. Box 789
  Cedar Rapids, IA 52406

- Baltimore City Head Start
  2330 St. Paul Street
  Baltimore, MD 21231

- Dane County Parent Council, Inc.
  802 Williamson Street
  Madison, WI 53703

- Coastal Community Action Program
  117 East Third Street
  Aberdeen, WA 98520

- Puget Sound Educational Service District
  400 Southwest 152nd Street
  Burien, WA 98166-2209

- Child Development Council of Franklin County
  398 South Grant
  Columbus, OH 43224

- Community Action Council for Lexington-Fayette,
    Bourbon, Harrison, and Nicholas Counties
  913 Georgetown Street
  P. O. Box 11610
  Lexington, KY 40576

Research

The Homeless Demonstration Programs included a mandated research component. Head Start plans to use the results of these studies to help design appropriate curricula and classroom environments for homeless children and to develop more individualized programs for families with special needs.

Preliminary research results have been reported. Sally A. Koblinsky and Elaine A. Anderson, Department of Family Studies, University of Maryland, College Park, completed a collaborative study with United Planning Organization Head Start in Washington, D.C., to examine how family variables influence the development and self-concept of homeless and permanently housed Head Start children [Koblinsky & Anderson 1993]. Koblinsky and Anderson evaluated the Bright Beginnings program at D.C.'s, Georgetown University.

References

Administration for Children, Youth, and Families (ACYF). (1992). *Homeless children and families: Information memorandum.* (Head Start Bureau, ADF-IM-92-12). Washington, DC: Author.

Koblinsky, S.A., & Anderson, E.A. (1993). Serving homeless children and families in Head Start. *Children Today, 22,* 19–23, 36.

A PPENDIXES

APPENDICES

A P P E N D I X

Safety Checklists

The following checklists provide guidelines for assessing the safety of shelter sites and playgrounds. Both checklists have been adapted and are reprinted with the permission of the Injury Prevention and Control Program, a division of the Massachusetts Department of Public Health.

The playground safety checklist is a compilation of suggested guidelines based on Consumer Product Safety Commission guidelines, international playground standards, and expert opinions from consultants in the field of playground safety.

Site Safety Checklist

General Environment

	Yes	No	NA	Comments
Floors are smooth and have nonskid surfaces.				
Pipes and radiators are inaccessible to children or are covered to prevent contact.				
Hot water temperature for washing hands is 110°–115° F or less.				
Electrical cords are out of children's reach and are kept out of doorways and traffic paths.				
Unused electrical outlets are covered by furniture or shock stops.				
Medicines, cleaners, and aerosols are locked away and inaccessible to children.				
Windows have screens that stay in place when pushed. Do not use expandable screens.				
Windows can be opened only 4 inches or less from the bottom.				
Drawers are kept closed to prevent tipping.				
Trash is covered at all times.				
Walls and ceilings are free of peeling paint and cracked or falling plaster.				

	Yes	No	NA	Comments
There is no friable, crumbly, asbestos being released into the air.				
The center has been inspected for lead paint.				
Miniblinds manufactured prior to 1996 have been replaced with lead-free miniblinds.				
There are no disease-bearing animals, such as cats, dogs, birds, hamsters, guinea pigs, lizards, or turtles.				
Children are supervised at all times.				

Equipment and Toys

	Yes	No	NA	Comments
Toys and play equipment are checked often for sharp edges, small parts, and sharp points.				
Toys are too large to fit completely into children's mouths and have no detachable parts.				
Lead-free paint is used on all painted toys and equipment.				
Hinges and joints are covered to prevent small fingers from being pinched or caught.				
Balloons are not allowed at the center.				
Riding toys are stable and well-balanced. All riders use helmets.				
Toys are put away when not in use.				

Equipment and Toys (continued)

	Yes	No	NA	Comments
Toy chests have lightweight lids or no lids at all.				
Art materials are nontoxic.				
Art materials are stored in original containers and locked away.				
Teaching aids, such as projectors, are put away when not in use.				
Curtains, pillows, blankets, and cloth toys are made of flame-resistant materials.				
There are no projectile toys, such as pop guns or darts.				

Hallways and Stairs

	Yes	No	NA	Comments
Stairs and stairways are free of boxes, toys, and other clutter.				
Stairways are well lit.				
The right-hand railings on stairs are at child height and do not wobble when held.				
There are railings or walls on both sides of stairways.				
Stairway gates are in place when appropriate.				
Closed doorways to unsupervised or unsafe areas are always locked, unless this prevents emergency evacuation.				

	Yes	No	NA	Comments
Staff members are able to watch for strangers entering the building.				
Kitchen				
Trash is kept away from areas where food is prepared or stored.				
Trash is stored away from furnaces and water heaters.				
Pest strips are not used. Pesticides are applied by certified pest-control professionals.				
Kitchens are not accessible to children unless there is constant adult supervision.				
Other cooking facilities or equipment are out of children's reach.				
Cleaners and other poisonous products are stored in original containers away from food and out of children's reach.				
Nonperishable foods are stored in labeled, insect-resistant containers.				
Perishable foods are stored in covered containers and refrigerated.				
Food-preparation surfaces are clean and free of cracks and chips.				
Eating utensils are free of cracks and chips.				

Kitchen (continued)

	Yes	No	NA	Comments
Electrical cords are placed where people will not trip over them or pull them.				
Sharp or hazardous cooking utensils, such as knives or glass, are not within children's reach.				
Pot handles are turned in toward the back of the stove during cooking.				
Fire extinguishers are reached easily in emergencies.				
All staff members know how to use fire extinguishers correctly.				

Bathrooms

	Yes	No	NA	Comments
Stable step stools are available when needed.				
Electrical outlets are covered with shock stops or outlet covers.				
Cleaning products, soaps, and disinfectants are locked away and out of children's reach.				
Floors are smooth and have nonskid surfaces.				
Trash containers are emptied daily and kept clean.				
Hot water temperature for washing hands is 110°–115° F.				

Emergency Preparation

	Yes	No	NA	Comments
Staff members understand their roles and responsibilities in case of emergencies.				
At least one staff person certified in first aid and infant and child CPR is present at all times.				
First aid kits are checked regularly for supplies and are easily accessible by staff members in emergencies.				
Smoke detectors and other alarms are checked regularly to make sure they are working.				
Each room and hallway has a fire escape route posted in clear view.				
Emergency procedures and telephone numbers are posted near each phone in clear view.				
Contact information for parents and guardians is near the phone, where it can be reached quickly.				
Poison control center stickers are on every telephone.				
All exits are clearly marked and free of clutter.				
Doors open in the direction of exit travel.				

Playground Safety Checklist

General Environment	Yes	No	NA	Comments
Suitable perimeter fences are provided.				
Seating—benches and outdoor tables—is in good condition.				
Trash receptacles are provided and located away from play areas.				
Poisonous plants are removed from play areas.				
Play areas have adequate shade.				
The entire play area can be seen easily for good supervision.				
Nuts, bolts, and screws are recessed, covered, or sanded smooth and level.				
Nuts and bolts are tight and cannot be loosened by hand.				
Metal equipment is free of rust and chipping paint.				
Wooden equipment is free of splinters and rough surfaces.				
All equipment is free of sharp edges.				
Ropes, chains, and cables are not frayed or worn.				

	Yes	No	NA	Comments
Equipment has not shifted or become bent.				
There is no corrosion where equipment comes into contact with ground surfaces.				
There are no "V" entrapment angles on any part of the equipment.				
Footings for equipment are stable and buried below ground level.				
The equipment is designed for the age and developmental levels of the children who will be using it.				

Ground Surfaces

	Yes	No	NA	Comments
Elevated play equipment, such as slides, swings, bridges, seesaws, and climbing apparatus, has 12 inches of impact-absorbing material underneath and extending 8 feet around the structure—such as sand, pea gravel (round 1/8-inch pellets), or wood chips. Wood chips and pea gravel are not acceptable for infant and toddler areas.				
Surfaces are checked at least weekly and raked to prevent them from becoming packed down and to remove hidden hazards such as litter, sharp objects, or animal feces.				

Ground Surfaces (continued)

	Yes	No	NA	Comments
Loose materials are replenished as needed to maintain adequate depth and coverage.				
There is no standing water on surfaces or inside equipment.				

Spacing

	Yes	No	NA	Comments
Swings have adequate clearance in both directions—twice the height of the swing both in front of and behind the stationary seat. This entire area should be covered with impact-absorbing material.				
Swings are at least 18 inches from each other and 28 inches away from the frame.				
Slides have 2.5 to 3 yards of space at the bottom.				
There is at least 8 feet between all equipment and fixed objects such as trees and buildings.				
Boundaries between equipment are visible to children—for instance, painted lines or low bushes.				
Play areas for activity play—such as bike riding or running games—are located away from areas for quiet activities, such as sandboxes or outdoor tables.				

Slides

Slides	Yes	No	NA	Comments
Slides are no more than 6 feet high.				
Slide ladders are angled at 50° to 75° and have handrails on both sides and flat steps.				
The top of the slide has a flat surface to help position children for sliding.				
The top of the slide has sufficient safety barriers to prevent side falls.				
Side rims are at least 4 inches high (5 inches for wave slides).				
The angle of sliding surfaces is no more than 40°.				
There is a flat surface at the bottom of the slide. If the slide is more than 4 feet high, the flat surface should be 16 inches in length.				
The bottom of the sliding surface is no more than 15 inches above the ground.				
There is a safety "run-off" zone of no less than 7.5 feet at the bottom of the slide.				
There are no circular slides in preschool areas.				

Slides (continued)

	Yes	No	NA	Comments
Sliding surfaces are not made of wood or fiberglass.				
For slides manufactured in several pieces, there are no gaps or rough edges in sliding surfaces.				
Sliding surfaces face away from the sun or are located in the shade.				
The steps on the slide are slip-resistant.				
Steps are regularly spaced, 7–11 inches apart, from top to bottom.				
Equipment is free from all other hazards.				

Climbing Equipment

	Yes	No	NA	Comments
Handholds stay in place when grasped.				
Equipment height does not exceed 2–3 feet for toddlers and 4 feet for 4- to 5-year-olds.				
Climbers have regularly spaced footholds, 7–11 inches apart, from top to bottom.				
There are easy, safe exits when children reach the top.				

	Yes	No	NA	Comments
Preschool equipment that is more than 30 inches above the ground has guardrails of 32 inches or higher—38-inch guardrails if school-age children use the equipment.				
Spaces between slats in barriers do not exceed 3.5 inches.				
Equipment is free from all other hazards.				
Swings				
Swing seats with back supports and safety bars are available for toddlers and children with disabilities.				
Swing seats are made of canvas, rubber, or other lightweight materials.				
There are no open-ended "S" hooks.				
Hanging rings are less than 5 inches or more than 10 inches in diameter—smaller or larger than a child's head.				
The point at which the chain or rope and the seat meet is designed to prevent hand or foot entrapment.				
Chain link openings do not exceed $^5/_{16}$ inches in diameter.				
Preschool swing seats are at a maximum height of 18 inches.				

Swings (continued)

	Yes	No	NA	Comments
Tire swings have a least a 24-inch safety zone between the support structure and the farthest extensions of swings.				
Tire swings have drainage openings every 5–6 inches.				
Tire swings are not made of steel-belted radial tires. Protruding steel belts can cause injuries.				
Plane swings, or gliders, have stable handholds, footholds, and seats.				
Equipment is free from all other hazards.				

Sandboxes

	Yes	No	NA	Comments
Sandboxes are located in shaded spots.				
Sand is checked and raked at least weekly for debris and to dry out.				
Sandboxes are covered at night to protect them from moisture and animal excrement.				
Sandboxes have proper drainage.				
Equipment is free from all other hazards.				

Rocking Equipment

	Yes	No	NA	Comments
Seating surfaces are less than 39 inches above the ground.				
No parts could cause pinching or crushing injuries.				
Handholds stay in place when grasped.				
Footrests stay in place.				
Equipment is free from all other hazards.				
All components of the equipment are secure and firmly fixed.				

Tunnels

	Yes	No	NA	Comments
Internal diameters of tunnels are at least 40 inches.				
Tunnels have two safe exits.				
Tunnels are designed to drain freely.				
Equipment is free from all other hazards.				

A P P E N D I X B

Volunteers' Roles in Shelter Programs

Pat Ward

The shelter child care programs surveyed by the author take advantage of the different abilities that volunteers have by using them in any combination of the following roles:

Working Directly with Children

- *Working as teachers and assistants*
    - Δ   in child care programs
    - Δ   on field trips
    - Δ   as tutors

- *Designing and helping with special events, such as*
    - Δ   birthday parties
    - Δ   holiday parties
    - Δ   recognition luncheons and dinners
    - Δ   community education events

- *Sharing special talents to enrich programs, such as*
    - Δ   music
    - Δ   art
    - Δ   dance
    - Δ   clowning
    - Δ   puppet making
    - Δ   storytelling
    - Δ   gardening with children
    - Δ   cooking

- *Improving children's health by providing*
  - Δ pediatric services
  - Δ mental health services
  - Δ dental services
  - Δ optometric services

Operations

- *Improving shelter facilities through*
  - Δ engineering
  - Δ contracting
  - Δ architectural services
  - Δ landscaping and flower planting
  - Δ cleaning and repair

- *Improving program operations by*
  - Δ organizing clothes and shoe closets
  - Δ collecting supplies
  - Δ taking cooks from centers to buy groceries
  - Δ picking up fresh fruit and milk
  - Δ maintaining and repairing toys
  - Δ making quilts, hats, and mittens
  - Δ providing transportation

Coordination and Management

- *Providing staff and volunteer training in*
  - Δ child development
  - Δ stress management
  - Δ discipline
  - Δ health and safety
  - Δ team building

- *Providing volunteer management by*
  - Δ coordinating volunteer activities
  - Δ acting as liaisons between boards, staff members, and volunteers

Governance and Advocacy

- *Serving on governing boards and committees that deal with*
  - Δ personnel matters
  - Δ financial matters
  - Δ public relations
  - Δ special events

- *Educating the public by*
  - Δ informing local government and state and national legislators about homeless people, their needs, and the causes of homelessness
  - Δ informing communities at large about homelessness to get people thinking and to encourage action

Sample Job Description for Volunteers

Family & Children's Service, Greensboro, North Carolina

Position	Child Care Worker
Reports to	Child Development Specialist
Job Role	To provide a psychologically and physically safe environment for children from violent homes. To provide opportunities to enhance self-esteem and encourage trust.
Responsibilities	1. Help plan and supervise age-appropriate activities: play, arts and crafts, games, toys, reading.
	2. Provide positive attention. Set appropriate limits and follow through.
	3. Assist the child development specialist in maintaining the physical environment.
Training	Family and Children's Service volunteer training—22 hours. Individualized, supervised training by staff members.
Time and Place	Clara House, Monday–Friday, 6:00–8:30 P.M. Other times to be arranged.
Commitment	One year, one shift per week.
Supervision	Monthly staff–volunteer meetings; weekly meetings with supervisor.

Qualifications

1. Experience working with children
2. Creativity and flexibility
3. Warmth and sensitivity to children of all ages
4. Willingness to learn and follow supervision
5. 18 years of age or older

A P P E N D I X D

Discipline Policy

Our House, Decatur, Georgia[1]

> This discussion, adapted from the discipline policy of Our House shelter, Decatur, Georgia, illustrates possible discipline policy issues. Experienced professionals should provide initial training for volunteers regarding discipline issues.

We at Our House use the term *discipline* to mean a corrective action to teach children a more appropriate behavior than the one they are exhibiting. Discipline at Our House never includes physical punishment, verbal abuse, humiliation, sarcasm, or long periods of time-out. No matter what the behavior of the child might be, no staff member, volunteer, or parent may spank, slap, scream at, or make fun of a child; this includes interactions between parents and their own children. Other forms of verbal abuse interfere with learning and with the development of a positive self-image. Encourage, praise, be positive!

Staff members will use the following techniques to help children in problem situations. If you spend time with the children as a volunteer or parent, you will be expected to use these ideas, too. Feel free to ask for help any time in handling misbehavior and to match the methods used by staff members and other adults in handling problem behaviors. Children learn to work and play within limits much more quickly when the adults in their environment try to deal with their misbehavior consistently in similar ways. Homeless children experience uncertainty many times, even chaos and fear, every evening as they enter a living space shared with others. Stress upon those children whom we serve produces behavior that runs the gamut from aggression, to withdrawal, to depression. Our role is to provide unconditional love in a consistent, safe environment so that children will know they are worthwhile simply because they are children. We direct those inappropriate behaviors into appropriate actions, and we

---

[1]   Our House, 711 Columbia Drive, Decatur, GA 30030

help the children find language to express their feelings. We remember that the stress upon these children may have slowed their cognitive and social development.

Situation 1

You have made a reasonable request of a child and the child refuses.

Response

Move quickly to the child and speak only to that child. Stoop or sit on a low chair so that you can have eye-to-eye contact with the child when you talk. Speak gently but firmly in short simple sentences. Restate the request as, "I need you to. . . ." Keep a sense of humor and keep repeating the statement.

Example 1

If the request has to do with clean-up, it often helps to break the task into small steps.

> **Caregiver:** Alyce, pick up the blocks, please.
>
> **Alyce:** I don't want to. (Or Alyce does nothing.)
>
> **Caregiver** (gently, but firmly): Alyce, I need you to pick up the blocks.

If Alyce does not comply, you might ask her to pick up a dozen blocks and help count them out.

> **Caregiver:** Alyce, I need you to pick up a dozen blocks—that's 12. I'll help count while you pick them up.

Praise the child for picking up the blocks. You might say to another adult in the child's presence, "Alyce picked up a dozen blocks."

Example 2

If a rule has been broken, such as throwing food on the floor, restate the rule before you ask the child to pick up the food. For example, Jonathan throws his toast on the floor and asks for more.

> **Caregiver:** Jonathan, we do not throw food on the floor. I need you to pick the toast up and put it in the garbage can, and then I'll get you another piece. (Repeat if necessary.)

Situation 2

A child is out of control. This includes a temper tantrum, running around the play area nonproductively, throwing toys, grossly misusing art materials, or antagonizing other children. In this situation, ask a teacher or caregiver for help. You might observe this way of handling the situation.

Response

Request that the child stop whatever action he or she is performing. If the behavior continues, ask the child to take some time out. It will probably be necessary to help the child leave the group. Continue a gentle but firm statement of the required behavior. You may have to sit with a child who is completely out of control, or you may be able to leave the child alone for a minute or two. When you return to the child, or when the child is calmer, ask what caused the problem. Explain simply and calmly why the behavior is unacceptable.

Example

Catrena has left several play areas this morning. She is currently playing in the kitchen. Soon, you notice the dishes being thrown in the air. You approach and pull up a chair.

> **Caregiver** (firmly): Catrena, we do not throw the dishes. I need you to stop.

Catrena grabs the rest of the kitchen toys and throws them on the floor.

> **Caregiver:** Catrena, you need to take time out.
>
> **Catrena:** No.
>
> **Caregiver:** Catrena, you need to take time out.

Gently lead or carry Catrena to the time-out area. Sit with her, if necessary. Limit this time to two or three minutes.

> **Caregiver:** Catrena, I've noticed that you just couldn't find what you wanted to play with this morning. I'll bet you are tired of trying things that don't work right.

Catrena's responses will vary. Lead her back to selecting an activity that can calm her: looking at a picture book, painting, or drawing an "I'm mad" picture. Encourage Catrena as she selects other ways to express her anger or frustration.

Situation 3

Two children are having a conflict.

Response

Ask them to sit down together with you to talk. You may have to do the talking if they are under age 3. Say, "We don't hit or push; we use words to tell other friends what is wrong." Have the children tell *each other* what happened. Ask them to look at each other and to speak to each other. When they have finished, you may have to explain what each did to cause the conflict. Keep the explanation short and simple. Ask each child to tell the other what he or she would like the other to do. Have each child say whether he or she will do what is requested. You may suggest that they say, "I'm sorry," or that they hug and make up, but never force this. They may not feel sorry. It is usually better to let the children figure out how to show they are ready to try again with each other.

Example

Emma has been playing with the road set and cars, and Robert comes over, rearranges her road plan, and takes her car. Emma screams and jerks the road section away. Get both children to put down the toys they are holding and sit beside you. Ask Emma to tell you what happened. Ask Robert to tell you what happened.

> **Caregiver:** Robert, you may not take a toy from someone who is playing with it. Would you like to help Emma build the road?
>
> **Robert:** Yes.
>
> **Caregiver:** Tell Emma that you would like to help her build the road.

After Robert and Emma's interchange, you prompt once more:

> Emma, tell Robert what he can do to help build your road. It takes many people working together to build a road.

Emma may refuse to allow Robert to play with her at all. The caregiver may respect her wishes and ask her to say that to Robert, or she may choose another way to deal with this situation.

If the children in conflict are toddlers, help them to find another acceptable activity. Distract a young child from a toy that the child is trying to take from another. You may encourage the children to share or to take turns, but remember that very young children are not developmentally ready to play cooperatively or to share. When toddlers hit or bite, they may be responding to aggression. Many toddlers move through a stage of biting or hair-pulling—it is developmental, not abnormal. Certainly, you must show disapproval and tell the children that they may not bite or hit, but it is never appropriate to respond with the behavior that you are trying to eliminate.

Situation 4

A child refuses to join the group activity or disrupts the group during a story or instructional time.

Response

As a volunteer, you may help by going to the child who refuses to join the group and asking the child to sit with you in the group. If you sit in the group and participate, the child may model your appropriate behavior and receive the positive attention he or she needs for doing so. If the child refuses to join the group, find a quiet activity that interests and calms the child. Sit with the child in a spot far enough from the group that others are not lured from the group to join you. Ask the child occasionally if he or she is ready to join you. If a child disrupts the group, wait for the caregiver to give you directions.

Keep a sense of humor. Moving external limits to internal limits and practicing self-discipline is a lifetime goal. Some children move more quickly than others toward that goal.

The children at Our House have an opportunity to experience our respect for their worth and to learn that there are alternatives to express feelings and productive ways to resolve conflict with others. Our hope is that each child will experience the joy of making and receiving acknowledgment for responsible choices in problem situations.

Look for good behavior; give encouragement for attempted good behavior; give praise for good behavior!

Responding to Difficult Situations

Nancy H. Emerson, Our House

This list, distributed to volunteers at Our House shelter in Decatur, Georgia, illustrates possible responses to difficult situations. Experienced professionals should provide initial training for volunteers on this problem.

Sometimes, we are faced with difficult situations with children, times when we aren't sure what to say or do. How do we respond? I have a few suggestions:

- Listen in an accepting way to what a child tells you.
- Don't tell the child that what he or she is talking about is "silly," "not true," or "not nice."
- Do not judge what or whom the child tells you about.
- Be prepared as much as possible for situations you know will arise, such as sex or death. Practice what you will say when the children ask you questions.
- Be sure you have as many facts as possible before doing or saying too much.
- Be honest. Don't ever tell a child something untrue or something you do not know to be true.
- Do not interfere in children's private conversations unless it is necessary to clear up distortions or calm fears.
- Ask others for help if you feel unable to deal with a situation.
- Don't tell a child more than he or she has asked for or more than you estimate the child can handle at the time.
- Some things we can say or do when hard situations arise:
  - Δ Repeat what the child has told you, with no judgment.

Δ   Give some simple words to the child's obvious feelings:

—   "I'll bet you were scared."

—   "Did that make you mad or sad?"

—   "I'll bet that was hard for you. It would be hard for me."

Δ   Express your sorrow when appropriate.

Δ   Ask a child, "Do you want to tell me more about that?" and accept a refusal if that is the child's answer.

Δ   Say, "I don't know, let me think about that," when asked about something and you are not sure how to respond.

Δ   Refer some questions (personal, family-related, religious) to the child's parents. "I think you should ask your mama about that." Then check with the mother to be sure the child gets an answer.

• Remember that the hard things are often the most important things in a child's life at a particular time. If they were not, they would not be so hard for us and the children to handle.

Volunteer Resources

Energize Inc.
5450 Wissahickon Avenue
Philadelphia, PA 19144-5221
800/395-9800
215/438-8342
FAX 215/438-0434

This organization stresses incorporating various media into the recruitment process. Their resources include publications such as *The (Help) I-Don't-Have-Enough-Time Guide to Volunteer Management, From the Top Down,* and *The Volunteer Recruitment Book,* and the poster, "7 Deadly Signs of Directing Volunteers." Energize also offers recordkeeping software for volunteers—*V.I.M., Volunteer Information Management*—and videotapes such as *Colleagues: The Volunteer/Employee Relationships* and *Together: Volunteer-to-Volunteer Relationships.* The organization's free *Volunteer Energy Resource Guide* is published annually. Energize's Web site is located at www.energize.com.

Four-One-One
7304 Beverly Street
Annandale, VA 22003
703/354-6270
FAX 703/941-4360

The national clearinghouse on voluntarism, Four-One-One serves community volunteer programs; national organizations; and agencies concerned with human services and community needs, such as elementary and secondary schools, colleges, universities, and libraries. It also provides comprehensive resources for planning, designing, and managing successful volunteer programs. One of its programs, Super Volunteers!, encourages young people to become involved in community service by using materials such as club kits, a newsletter, and a volunteer board game to increase youth interest. It has an extensive directory on voluntarism, called *Volunteer America: The Directory of Organizations, Training, Programs, and Publications,* which lists over 5,000 local and national volunteer organizations.

Independent Sector
1828 L Street NW
Washington, DC 20036
202/223-8100
FAX 202/426-0580
This is a nonprofit coalition of nearly 800 corporations, foundations, and voluntary organizations interested in philanthropy and voluntary action nationwide. It publishes a monthly newsletter, *UPDATE,* as well as several other publications, including *What It Means to Volunteer: Lessons from America's Youth, Volunteers in Action,* and *Passing the Tradition of Service to Future Generations.*

National Center for Nonprofit Boards
2000 L Street NW, Suite 510
Washington, DC 20036-4907
800/883-6262
202/452-6262
FAX 202/452-6299
This resource center for volunteer boards of directors undertakes research projects and is currently publishing a series of manuals and books on effective board operations, including *The Ten Basic Responsibilities of Nonprofit Boards* and *Creating and Renewing Advisory Boards: Strategies for Success.*

The Points of Light Foundation
Information Services
1737 H Street NW
Washington, DC 20006
202/223-9186
FAX 202/223-9256
The Points of Light Foundation is an independent, nonprofit organization whose mission is to motivate leaders of organizations in all sectors and at all levels of society. It seeks to mobilize its members for community service projects aimed at alleviating the alarming social problems threatening America's future. The foundation issues a quarterly magazine, *Voluntary Action Leadership;* has a catalog of volunteer recognition items; and produces publications on volunteer management, such as *The Great Trainer's Guide: How To Train (Almost) Anyone To Do (Almost) Anything!* It also has a toll-free number through which prospective volunteers can find volunteer centers with corresponding interests in their communities (800/879-5400).

The Support Center
2001 0 Street NW
Washington, DC 20036
202/833-0300
FAX 202/857-0077

The center matches corporate volunteers with nonprofit organizations to fulfill their management, accounting, fundraising, training, and resource needs through the Volunteers for Community Service Program. The center recruits managers, accountants, and other professionals and technical experts to serve on boards of directors or to assist organizations on a volunteer basis with specific, short-term problems. The center coordinates and directs all aspects of Volunteers for Community Service, working directly with each organization to define its needs and find volunteers with appropriate skills to meet them. The process also involves meeting with volunteers and organizations to discuss what needs to be done and having volunteers prepare work plans that are acceptable to organizations before volunteers begin work.

Annotated Bibliography

To help you develop activity programs for children in shelters (see Chapter 5), following is a list of basic early childhood materials, published sources of activities for preschool and school-age children, and numerous resources specifically designed for children in shelters. Select activities from many sources to fit the needs of the children in your program. Since the children will be changing frequently and will be of various ages and abilities, we recommend a variety of open-ended materials and activities.

For Children Age 3 and Under

Cryer, D., Harms, T., & Bourland, B. (1987). *Active Learning for Infants*. Menlo Park, CA: Addison-Wesley Publishing.

Cryer, D., Harms, T., & Bourland, B. (1987). *Active Learning for Ones*. Menlo Park, CA: Addison-Wesley Publishing.

Cryer, D., Harms, T., & Bourland, B. (1988). *Active Learning for Twos*. Menlo Park, CA: Addison-Wesley Publishing.

Cryer, D., Harms, T., & Bourland, B. (1988). *Active Learning for Threes*. Menlo Park, CA: Addison-Wesley Publishing.

Cryer, D., Harms, T., & Ray, A. (1996). *Active Learning for Fours*. Menlo Park, CA: Addison-Wesley Publishing.

Cryer, D., Harms, T., & Ray, A. (1996). *Active Learning for Fives*. Menlo Park, CA: Addison-Wesley Publishing.

> The *Active Learning Series* contains planning guides and activities for infants and preschoolers through age 5. Activities are organized by developmental levels in four sections: Activities for Listening and Talking, Activities for Physical Development, Creative Activities, and Activities for Learning from the World Around Them. Activities are designed to use commonly available materials.

Gonzalez-Mena, J. (1990). *Infant/Toddler Caregiving. A Guide to Routines*. Sacramento: California Department of Education.

> This volume is part of a training program for caregivers of infants and toddlers, published by the California Department of Education. It includes detailed suggestions for making caregiving routines convenient and enjoyable for caregivers and good for children.

Honig, A.S., & Lally, J.R. (1981). *Infant Caregiving: A Design for Training*. Syracuse, NY: Syracuse University Press.

> This detailed training program includes ideas for activities to use with infants. In addition, it covers stages of infant development and deals with caregivers' practical concerns, such as assigning babies to caregivers, recordkeeping, and working with parents.

Parks, S. (Ed.). (1988). *HELP . . . at Home. Based on the Hawaii Early Learning Profile (HELP). Activity Sheets for Parents*. Palo Alto, CA: VORT Corporation.

This guide provides activities to teach skills in six developmental areas. It is designed for use with children operating at the birth-to-age-3 level. Staff members working with children in shelters will find the section on social-emotional development particularly helpful.

Sparling, J., & Lewis, I. (1981). *Learningames for the First Three Years: A Guide to Parent/Child Play*. New York: Berkley Books.

This book presents games based on infant development. It contains checklists for easy recordkeeping. The games use materials found in most homes and many shelters.

For 4- and 5-Year-Old Children

Derman-Sparks, L., & the A.B.C. Task Force (1991). *Anti-Bias Curriculum: Tools for Empowering Young Children*. Washington, DC: National Association for the Education of Young Children.

This book is for adults who work with children. It presents ways to reduce, handle, and eliminate biases against people of color and cultures other than their own and against people with different abilities.

McCracken, J.B. (Ed.). (1990). *Helping Children Love Themselves and Others: A Professional Handbook for Family Day Care*. Washington, DC: The Children's Foundation.

Designed for use in family child care, this book contains multicultural and anti-bias activities for use with children under age 5. Many of these activities are appropriate for shelters.

Mitchell, A., & David, J. (Eds.). (1992). *Explorations with Young Children: A Curriculum Guide from the Bank Street College of Education*. Mt. Rainier, MD: Gryphon House.

This book presents the approach to teaching young children developed at the Bank Street College of Education in New York City. Rather than a cookbook of activities, it is a method of developing curriculum by combining a knowledge of how children grow and develop with observations of children in your program.

Veitch, B., & Harms, T. (1980). *Cook and Learn: A Child's Cook Book*. Menlo Park, CA: Addison-Wesley Publishing.

This is a children's cookbook with single-portion pictorial recipes that is a teaching aid on learning-through-cooking with children.

Clear, simple, and enjoyable, the single-portion recipes develop sound nutrition principles and awareness of foods from many cultures.

Williams, L.R., & DeGaetano, Y. (1985). *ALERTA: A Multicultural, Bilingual Approach to Teaching Young Children*. Menlo Park, CA: Addison-Wesley Publishing Company.

This curriculum was developed for use in Head Start. Its focus is on building on the interests of children, the cultures of their families, and the specific elements of the surrounding environments. This is not a step-by-step curriculum, but a philosophy of using children's own experiences to design programs.

York, S. (1991). *Roots & Wings: Affirming Culture in Early Childhood Programs*. St. Paul, MN: Toys 'n Things Press.

Chapter 5 in this book is designed to help plan curriculum units on cultural diversity. Examples of activities include exploring the concept of skin color; similarities and differences of physical characteristics such as eyes and hair; exploring racial constancy (When I grow up, I'm going to be white, or black, or brown.); and feelings. Chapter 7 examines the development of racial and cultural awareness from infancy through age 9 and discusses how prejudice is formed.

For School-Age Children

Blau, R., Brady, E.H., Bucher, I., Hiteshew, B., Zavitovsky, A., & Zavitovsky, D. (1985). *Activities for School-Age Child Care*. Washington, DC: National Association for the Education of Young Children.

This book offers suggestions for materials and activities in arts and crafts, woodworking, cooking, and dramatic play for use with children ages 5 to 10 in settings outside of school and home, primarily child care centers.

Burton, L., & Karoda, K. (1991). Arts Play: Creative Activities in Art, Music, Dance, and Drama for Young Children. Menlo Park, CA: Addison-Wesley Publishing Company.

Includes 100 creative activities for individual and group use. Although some activities require more space than most shelters set aside for children, many can be adapted to shelter environments. Most activities can be completed in short periods of time. Because many children in shelters have delayed large-muscle (gross-motor) skill development, the music and dance activities will be particularly helpful.

For Homeless Children

Ennes, J.B. (1991). *Connecting: Meeting the Needs of Formerly Homeless Pre-School Children.* **New York: Child Care, Inc.**

Connecting is a training curriculum for child care staff members working with formerly homeless preschool children. It contains a section on appropriate activities and materials. Language development is built into all activities. Wherever possible, suggested activities are part of the normal routine of life in a shelter—making snacks, table talk, listening, writing children's stories, taking pictures, keeping weather charts, using magnets, setting tables, and recycling. Activities can be adapted easily to different ages and stages of development.

Gundy, J. (1984). *ACTIVITIES . . . More Than Keeping the Children Busy: A Therapeutic Curriculum for Children's Services in Shelters for Battered Women.* **Fayetteville, AR: Project for Victims of Family Violence, Inc.**

This activities manual, written for volunteers and child advocates working in shelters for battered women, contains activities for building children's self-esteem, for helping children identify and deal with their feelings, and for looking into the children's community. It also describes dangers in shelter environments and helps children learn to say good-bye to old friends.

Occupational Therapy Department, Virginia Treatment Center for Children. (1989). *Activities for Moms and Their Kids.* **Richmond, VA: Author**

This manual was written by the Occupational Therapy Department, Virginia Treatment Center for Children, for the Richmond Mental Health Clinic's Homeless Children and Families Project. It was designed specifically for use in shelters and offers active games and quiet table activities that can be completed in an hour or less and that require a minimal amount of set-up and clean-up time. Group activities or projects focus on socialization and cooperative skills.

Patterson, S. (1990). *I Wish the Hitting Would Stop: A Workbook for Children Living in Violent Homes.* **Fargo, ND: Red Flag, Green Flag Resources.**

This book is designed for people working with elementary-age children who live or have lived in homes where their mothers have been physically abused. Each page presents the child's point of view and helps children talk about, explore, and cope with their feelings. It also deals with issues of safety and getting help.

About the Authors

Jean Bombardier, M.S.W., is a senior grants and contracts specialist, Department of Health and Human Services, Seattle, Washington.

Sandra Botstein, M.D., is a pediatrician with the North Raleigh Pediatric Group and lives in Chapel Hill, North Carolina.

Rachel Fesmire, M.A., is the president and chief executive officer of Family and Children's Services, Greensboro, North Carolina.

Mary Foster, B.S., is an early intervention specialist with Guilford County Mental Health–Early Intervention Services, Greensboro, North Carolina.

Pat Gallagher, M.S., is the director of The Ark, Episcopal Social Ministries, Baltimore, Maryland.

Thelma Harms, Ph.D., is the director of curriculum development, Frank Porter Graham Child Development Center, University of North Carolina at Chapel Hill, and a research professor at the university's School of Education.

Tovah Klein, Ph.D., is an assistant professor of psychology and director of the Barnard Center for Toddler Development, Barnard College, Columbia University, New York, New York.

Robin Mauney, M.S.W., is the executive director of REACH, Murphy, North Carolina.

Andra M. McBain, B.A., is the executive director of the Dallas Jewish Coalition for the Homeless, Dallas, Texas.

Janice Molnar is the acting co-deputy director for human development and reproductive health, Asset Building and Community Development Program, Ford Foundation, New York, New York.

Beverly A. Mulvihill, Ph.D., is an assistant professor, Department of Maternal and Child Health, School of Public Health, University of Alabama at Birmingham.

Adele Richardson Ray, M.Ed., is a social research associate with the Frank Porter Graham Child Development Center, University of North Carolina at Chapel Hill.

Pam Rolandelli, Ph.D., is a training coordinator at the North Carolina Head Start Learning Center, Chapel Hill, North Carolina.

Pat Ward, M.S., is a senior associate with the Association of Junior Leagues International, New York, New York.

Marie Weil, D.S.W., is the director of the Community Social Work Program and a professor at the School of Social Work, University of North Carolina at Chapel Hill.

Evelyn Williams, M.S.W., is a clinical assistant professor, School of Social Work, University of North Carolina at Chapel Hill.